I0818869

PAVAN BAJWA

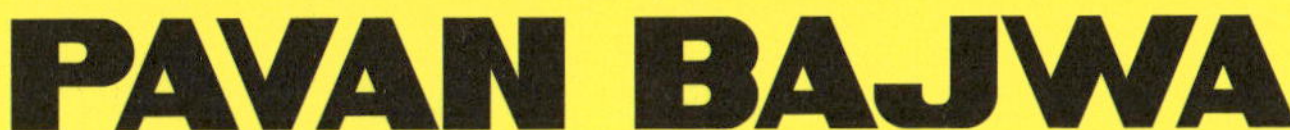

मिशन MISSION MASALA मसाला

EAT INDIA

photography
Studio Legein

creative direction
Olivier Smets

TASTE THE SPICY
INDIAN CUISINE

Lannoo

MISSION

If you had told me ten years ago that a few late-night curry experiments after work would spiral into four restaurants, food trucks, a full festival setup, three takeaway curry clubs, brewing our own beers and producing our own rum... I'd have laughed. But not because it sounded crazy. Just because it somehow made total sense.

And here we are.

I (Pavan) grew up in the UK in a loud, North Indian household where food was a love language. My mum's kitchen was always buzzing, pressure cookers hissing, spices toasting, something bubbling away on the back burner. By the time I could reach the counter, I was already learning how to layer flavours, not just throw things in a pan. I ended up studying menswear design, and yes, I like things to look good. That same design eye now shapes everything we do at Mission Masala, from the food to the setting and the atmosphere in our spaces.

Mission Masala was never about doing classic Indian food. As for a lot of kids growing up in two cultures, the food at home was always a bit of both. When my mum cooked Indian food, she had to make it a bit more Western so we'd eat it. But even then, she always had to tweak it: my dad's refusal to eat anything without spice meant Indian flavours made their way into everything.

That kind of mash-up became my normal. And when I moved to Belgium for work, people kept asking me where they could find a good Indian restaurant. The thing was, though, that I never had a solid answer. So I started inviting them over instead. I'd cook, we'd eat, and I'd show them how to make it themselves. Those cosy evenings were filled with booze, experiments, laughter, and the kind of energy that carried us late into the night.

Meeting Tim was a game changer! With his love of flavour, colour and going big, we clicked instantly, teamed up, and haven't stopped since.

Born and raised in Antwerp, he had been building mixes way before he ever touched a spice jar. As a DJ he'd been spinning records and packing dancefloors for over two decades. His brain just knows how to mix things, whether it's genres, beats or flavours. Before Mission Masala, he co-founded Barrio Cantina, one of Belgium's OG food truck festivals, so street food was already in his blood.

It progressed from there: small home catering gigs, street parties and, eventually, a food truck.

From a side hustle to where we are today, we've learned (and burned) a lot along the way, but one thing has stayed the same: we cook food we love to eat. Food that's bold, messy, colourful, and made to be shared. Not traditional, but always rooted in flavour and feeling.

Mission Masala is our love child, born from two very different backgrounds, but one shared obsession: food and drinks that hit hard and make people feel something.

This book is our journey on paper. A mix of old-school recipes and mad new fusions. The dishes that brought us together, fed our friends, and filled our restaurants with returning regulars.

To our team, our day-one regulars, our festival family, and everyone who ever asked for "just one more samosa", thank you. You made this real.

Now grab a pan. Open something cold. Let's cook.

With love, spice, and a lot of mess,

Pavan (& Tim)

Mission Masala

सॉसेस, चुटनेस & कंडीमेंट्स
SAUCES, CHUTNEYS & CONDIMENTS
25

ब्रेकफास्ट
BREAKFAST
39

शेयरिंग स्नैक्स
SNACKS
59

करी क्लब
CURRY CLUB
87

बॉम्बे बीबीक्यू
BOMBAY BBQ
121

देस्सेर्ट्स
DESSERTS
153

कॉकटेल्स & कूलर्स
COCKTAILS & COOLERS
165

रास्ते में
ON THE ROAD
HOW OUR FOOD TRUCKS STARTED THE FIRE

From backyard brainstorm to festival icons

Before the restaurants, before the rum, before the chaos of full-service kitchens, there was one beat-up Constructam caravan and a whole lot of spice.

It all kicked off when Tim, back then a DJ and co-founder of Barrio Cantina, Belgium's first major food truck festival, came home just weeks after the first successful edition with a beaten-up vintage caravan and a glint in his eye.

It became our first Curry Cruiser. We ripped out the guts, rebuilt it from scratch, added a kitchen and, just a few weeks later, launched it at the next edition of Barrio Cantina.

From the start, it wasn't just about the food, it was about creating a full experience. We've always been obsessed with giving people more than a plate of curry: colour, sound, smoke, spice, and a hit of energy that triggers all the senses. Festivals and restaurants alike, we wanted guests to catch a glimpse of the vibrancy and visual chaos India has to offer, but always through our Mission twist. That's why we teamed up with Belgian graphic designer Olivier Smets. He'd never set foot in India, but his love for fonts and obsession with detail meant he got it. Together we built the Mission Masala visual language: loud, bold, layered, an extension of the food itself. Whether it's a napkin design, a food stand that looks like a roadside shack in India, a menu cover or even the toilets in our restaurant, your eyes will never rest because there's always something new to discover.

GENT JAZZ FESTIVAL, OUR FIRST BIG BREAK

We rolled up with colour, soul and desi street food. And people got it. The queue was long, the energy was high, and the message was clear: this was more than food.

But we also noticed something else:

At every festival, the top-selling trucks had one thing in common: BBQ smoke, showcooking and fire.

So we jumped on it – Indian flavours, cooked on coals and packed into burgers.

BOMBAY BBQ

That's when Bombay BBQ was born and that's when Guido came on board. Back then a Dutch intern at the Polé Polé festivals, Guido jumped onboard, literally. Together we sketched out the concept for truck #2: Rougher, hotter and louder.

We rolled in with our OG Indian street burgers like Bombay Badboy (lamb seekh), Queen La Tikka (Tandoori chicken) and Pow Pow Paneer (Paneer tikka).

All with our Mission twist, loaded with typical Indian sauces, desi mayos and crunchy toppings. Saucy, spicy, and perfectly festival-proof.

Since then, we've been tearing up the food truck scene, hitting the biggest festivals across Belgium and the Netherlands, slinging thousands of curries, burgers, samosas and naan rolls from open grills under neon lights.

We've fed muddy ravers and early risers. We've served in sun, rain, and once in a literal hailstorm. We've watched people bite into a samosa and close their eyes in slow motion. And we're not stopping anytime soon.

The food truck is where Mission Masala started, and where the fire still burns brightest.

A massive shoutout to the festivals that opened their grounds to us, to the diehard fans who meet us year after year on the road, and to the Mission army, the beasts who grind it out with relentless force, through blood, smoke and BBQ.

Barrio Cantina
Best Kept Secret
Cactus
Core Festival
Couleur Café
Dekmantel
Down the Rabbit Hole
Dranouter
Extrema Outdoor
Gent Jazz
Jazz Middelheim
Kasserol
Lentekabinet
Live is Live
Mad Festival
Mysteryland
Paaspop
Paradise City
Pinkpop
Pukkelpop
Solar
Tomorrowland
Us by Night
Voodoo Village
We Can Dance

THE MISSION MASALA ESSENTIALS

Spices, staples, and all the good stuff. Your flavour HQ. This is where the real prep begins.

Indian food isn't about rules. It's about rhythm. Heat, sizzle, spice, taste, repeat.

This chapter is your starter pack for navigating the Indian kitchen, from understanding spices to building bold flavours and remixing them like a pro.

FRESH INGREDIENTS

Everyday staples for your base or finishing touches.

TAMATAR

TOMATOES
Fresh or tinned; used for tang and body in sauces.

PYAAZ

ONIONS
Brown for deep curries, sliced for grills, chopped for tarka.

ADRAK-LAHSUN

GINGER–GARLIC PASTE
1:1 blend; foundational for curries and marinades.

DHANIYA PATTA

PUDINA

CURRY PATTA

FRESH CORIANDER
Finisher, adds brightness and lift.

FRESH MINT
For chutneys, raitas or grilled meats.

FRESH CURRY LEAF
Use fresh if possible; add to hot oil to wake up dhals, chutneys, and South Indian bases.

MIRCH

RAWAT GREEN CHILLIES
Suits Indian cooking the best & brings fresh heat. Slit length ways or chopped very small. Don't remove the seeds, that's a waste.

BIG RED CHILLIES
For garnishing.

NIMBU

LIME OR LEMON
Add at the end to cut through richness of both curries and anything BBQ'd.

ESSENTIAL WHOLE SPICES

Tempering these in hot oil releases deep aromas and forms the backbone of many dishes.

ELAICHI

GREEN CARDAMOM
Sweet, floral and fragrant.

JEERA

CUMIN SEEDS
Nutty, earthy and deeply aromatic.

RAI

MUSTARD SEEDS
Pungent, sharp; pop them in oil to release bitterness.

BADI ELAICHI

BLACK CARDAMOM
Smoky, earthy, adds depth to slow-cooked dishes.

LAUNG

CLOVES
Warm, intensely aromatic, used whole or ground.

DALCHINI

CINNAMON STICKS
Sweet, woody spice for curries and biryanis.

SOOKHI LAL MIRCH

DRIED RED CHILLIES
Smoky heat and a gorgeous red hue.

METHI DANA

FENUGREEK SEEDS
Slightly bitter, toasty and maple-like when cooked.

TEJ PATTA

BAY LEAVES
Mild, earthy, used in rice dishes and long simmers.

CORE GROUND SPICES

Add them to build layers of flavour or finish a dish with warmth and aroma.

4.

7.

8.

1.	**TURMERIC POWDER (Haldi)** Earthy and golden, foundational in most Indian dishes.	6.	**AMCHOOR (Dry mango powder)** Tangy and sharp, perfect for chaat or legumes.
2.	**CORIANDER POWDER (Dhaniya powder)** Citrus, nutty and mellow.	7.	**CHAAT MASALA** Funky, sour, salty and spicy – essential for finishing snacks.
3.	**CUMIN POWDER (Jeera powder)** Deeper and smokier than the seeds.	8.	**DRIED FENUGREEK LEAVES (Kasuri methi)** Crushed at the end; earthy, bitter, aromatic.
4.	**KASHMIRI CHILLI POWDER (Deggi mirch)** Vibrant red, mild heat, more for colour.	9.	**CINNAMON POWDER** Warm, sweet-spicy, adds depth to curries, desserts and drinks.
5.	**GARAM MASALA** A final flourish: warm blend of clove, cardamom, cinnamon, etc.	10.	**ROASTED CUMIN POWDER** Toasty, fragrant and aromatic.

LENTILS, FLOURS & GRAINS

BASMATI RICE
Long-grain, aromatic; for pulao, biryani and sides.

ATTA (Whole wheat flour)
For roti, paratha and wraps.

GRAM FLOUR (Besan)
Nutty and binding; used in batters, marinades and pakoras.

RED LENTILS (Masoor dal)
Quick-cooking, soft and comforting.

YELLOW SPLIT MOONG DAL
Mild and light.

SALTS

HIMALAYAN PINK SALT
Mild, mineral-rich, subtly sweet.

MALDON SMOKED SALT
Flaky, smoky, mellow.

BLACK SALT (Kala namak)
Sulphuric, funky, perfect for chaats and drinks.

TABLE SALT
Fine, clean, everyday for gravies and anything with a long simmer.

OILS, FATS & DAIRY

Used to build richness, carry spice or mellow heat.

GHEE
Buttery and nutty; finish dishes or cook special rice dishes with it.

MUSTARD OIL
(Sarson ka tel)
Pungent and sharp; brilliant for marinades and Bengali cooking.

NEUTRAL OIL
(Sunflower or vegetable)
Base for frying and general use.

YOGHURT
(Dahi)
For chutneys, raitas, or grilled meats.

BUTTER
Used in creamy dishes like butter chicken and paneer.

PICKLES

Store-bought Indian pickles – tangy, spicy, ready to eat; buy, try, and experiment by mixing into mayo, yoghurt, or sauces for a flavour kick.

OTHER CLASSICS

GUR

JAGGERY
Unrefined sugar; balances sourness or heat.

IMLI

TAMARIND PASTE
Sour and sticky; used in chutneys and South Indian curries.

PANEER
Fresh Indian cheese from De Zuivelarij; for grills, curries or stir-fries.

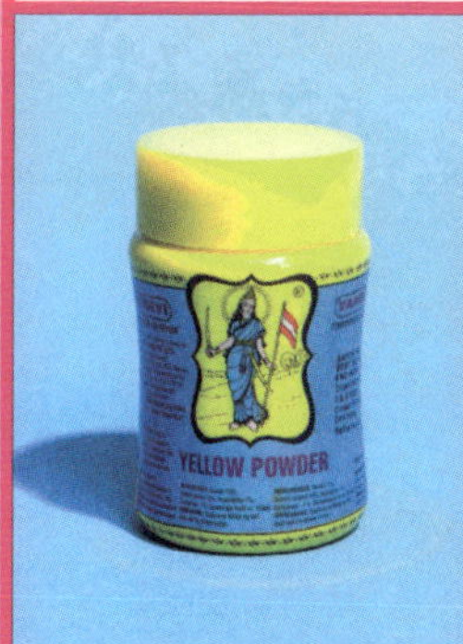

ASAFOETIDA
Pungent, savoury, umami-rich; adds depth to dals and vegetable dishes.

ROSE WATER
Floral, delicate, aromatic; used in desserts, drinks and biryanis.

INDIAN SNACK SHELF
Dry, crunchy, ready-to-eat snacks like Bombay mix, sev, and more. Ready-made savoury mixes for instant nibbling or adding a crunch topping to any dish.

CASHEW NUTS
Soaked and blended for creamy sauces (e.g. butter chicken).

CREAM OR COCONUT MILK
Optional richness for certain curries or South Indian dishes.

दुकान
SHOP

To cook these recipes properly, you'll need the right spices. It only takes one trip to an Indian shop to stock up, and to make it easier, I've included my recommended shops in different cities. The pantry list in the book is a great guide, so if you're unsure, take the book with you to your local South Asian or Indian store. The staff will be more than happy to help you find everything you need.

What's even more exciting is discovering everything else from ready-to-eat Indian snacks to beautifully designed packaging that pulls you in only to uncover a pantry of possibilities and ingredients waiting to be explored.

ANTWERP
Rahman.S Supermarket
Sint-Elisabethstraat 14
2060 Antwerpen
GHENT
Himalaya Exotic Market
Brusselsepoortstraat 110
9000 Gent
BRUSSELS
Express Afro Indian
Bd du Midi 98
1000 Bruxelles
AMSTERDAM
Authentic India
Eerste Van Swindenstraat 16
1093 GD Amsterdam
ROTTERDAM
Singh's mini market,
Indian Store
Vierambachtsstraat 137B
3022 AL Rotterdam

मसाला
INDIAN SOULFOOD

7,50.
Kilo

LET'S COOK

The Mission Masala cookbook is more than just a collection of recipes; it's a guide to cooking with confidence. Instead of simply telling you what to cook, it shows you how to cook, with masterclasses woven throughout the book. You'll learn the skills behind the dishes: how to fold a paratha, stuff a samosa, and build marinades that work for anything from oven roasts to barbecue nights. Each chapter is built around essential building blocks you can use again and again, until they become staples in your everyday kitchen. Just as we put Indian food on the map in Belgium and brought it into homes through our Curry Clubs, now we're handing the tools over to you – to play, experiment, and discover your own favourite flavours at home.

This book is also an invitation to experiment across chapters. Mix and mash things together, try combinations that feel unexpected, and don't be afraid to freestyle. Trial and error is where the magic happens – you'll stumble on your own favourite flavour profiles, and find the levels of heat, salt and spice that feel just right for you.

Think of these recipes as starting points, not strict rules. One night you might turn a chutney into a marinade, the next you'll use a curry base to bring life to leftovers. The point is to have fun, cook with curiosity, and create food that feels like yours.

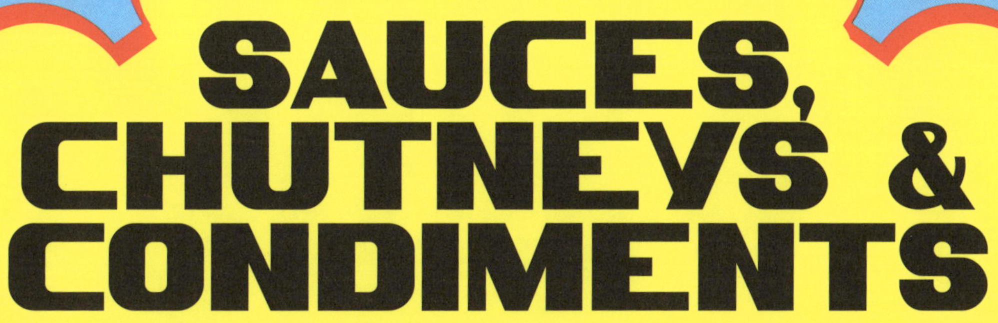

SAUCES, CHUTNEYS & CONDIMENTS

SPICE. DRIZZLE. SPREAD. DUNK. REPEAT.

सॉसेस, चुटनेस & कंडीमेंट्स

Sauces, chutneys and mayos are the foundation of so many of our dishes – especially at festivals. They're the reason we love street food so much. A little messy, a lot of flavour and, honestly, the only way to turn something into a proper guilty pleasure. With Mission cooking, the condiments are never an afterthought – they're the punchlines, the flavour bombs, the bits people remember. And the best part: they're easy to prep, perfect for pimping up leftovers, and you can mix and match them with pretty much anything you're eating – it doesn't even have to be Indian.

25

10.
3.
8.
9.
2.
6.
7.

1. TAMARIND CHUTNEY
p. 28
2. MANGO CHUTNEY
p. 29
3. MANGO MAYO
p. 29
4. APRICOT CHUTNEY
p. 30
5. CORIANDER & MINT CHUTNEY
p. 31
6. CORIANDER & MINT MAYO
p. 31
7. SWEET FENNEL CHUTNEY
p. 32
8. KARMA KETCHUP
p. 33
9. CURRY LEAF TARTAR
p. 34
10. COCONUT SAMBOL
p. 35
11. PICKLED DAIKON IN NORTH INDIAN PICKLING LIQUID
p. 37
1.
5.
11.
4.

TAMARIND CHUTNEY

A sweet and tangy condiment that can be made at various levels of thickness, sweetness and spice. I call it Indian ketchup. Traditionally used in chaats, this one brings life to anything it touches. A dipping sauce, a taco topper, a lively chaat, or just eat it with a spoon (we won't judge). We use this on our samosas, or even drizzle it on fried eggs. This chutney also makes a killer glaze for BBQ or grilled aubergine.

INGREDIENTS

400 g seedless tamarind pulp (1 packet)
800 ml water
200 g jaggery or brown sugar (preferably jaggery)
50 g tomato ketchup
2 tsp cumin seeds, toasted and ground
2 tsp fennel seeds, toasted and crushed
1 tsp chilli powder (or start with ½ tsp and add more later if you don't want your chutney too spicy)
1 tsp of black salt (or sea salt)

METHOD

In a small saucepan, add the tamarind pulp and water. Bring to a simmer and break up the pulp with a spoon. Let it bubble for 10–15 minutes until it thickens slightly and the pulp separates from the fibres (you want the pulp to have dissolved into the water).

Strain, leaving a smooth paste. Discard leftover fibres.

In a pan, add the extracted tamarind paste, the jaggery, spices and salt. Simmer again for 10 minutes until all flavours have combined and you have a sticky, sweet and tangy paste. Remove from the heat and stir in the ketchup.

Cool completely and store in a jar in the fridge.

Mission notes

For complex flavours: add a splash of date syrup or date paste, or throw in a couple of cardamom pods, 1–2 bay leaves, a cinnamon stick and 1–2 dried red chillies (remove these before storing, otherwise they will make the chutney bitter).

STORAGE

Keep in the fridge for up to a month.
Keep in the freezer for up to 3 months.

Tip:
Use an ice cube tray to freeze in handy portions.

MANGO CHUTNEY

Killer with fried snacks, grilled meats, or just dolloped on cheese toasties. Use this chutney to bring anything to life. This recipe can pretty much be adapted to any of your favourite fruits; peaches in summer, figs in autumn, whatever you've got. Or take the shortcut: grab your favourite jam (yes, even strawberry or pineapple) and give it a quick lift with the spices listed below.

INGREDIENTS

2–3 tbsp neutral oil (sunflower or rapeseed)
½ tsp fresh ginger, finely minced
1 small garlic clove, finely minced
1 small red chilli, sliced (optional; you can add more or less depending on your preference)
1 tsp nigella seeds
1 tsp ajwain seeds
1 tsp cumin seeds
1 tsp fennel seeds
½ teaspoon salt
a small pinch of turmeric
900 g ripe mango, peeled and diced (about 3 large mangos or the same weight frozen and thawed)
200 g white sugar
110 ml cider vinegar

METHOD

Heat the oil in a small saucepan over medium heat. Add the ginger, garlic and chilli (if using) and sauté for a minute until fragrant.

Stir in all the seeds. Toast them for 30 seconds, just enough to release their aromas. Add salt and turmeric. Stir for a couple of seconds.

Add the mango, sugar and vinegar. Stir well to coat everything in the spices.

Bring it all to a boil, then drop the heat and simmer uncovered for 25–35 minutes.

Stir occasionally until it thickens to a glossy, jammy chutney.

Let it cool, then spoon into a clean jar and try not to eat it all before it hits the fridge.

STORAGE

Store in a sealed jar.

Keep in the fridge for up to 2 months.

MANGO MAYO

Sweet, spicy, and an absolute crowd-pleaser.

INGREDIENTS

200 g good-quality mayo
40 g mango chutney (see above)
½ tsp garam masala
1 tbsp finely chopped jalapeños (pickled from a jar or can)
salt to taste

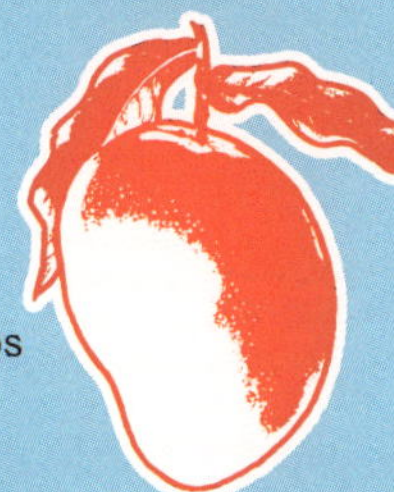

METHOD

Mix everything together until smooth and slightly speckled. Chill before using to let the flavours settle. If you can take the heat, add more jalapeños.

Mission notes

For added depth: while it's simmering, throw in a handful of raisins, a splash of dark rum, or a small pinch of ground cardamom, ground cloves and ground cinnamon.

Blitz the chutney if you like it smooth or leave it chunky to keep more texture (we love it chunky). If you prefer smaller chunks, use a masher to squash the mixture into your preferred consistency.

Want it hotter? Add a pinch of chilli powder or chilli flakes.

APRICOT CHUTNEY

Big on flavour, small on effort. Sweet, tangy, and just the right amount of spice. Great with grilled meats, roasted veggies, kebabs, samosas or a sharp cheese.

INGREDIENTS

250 g dried apricots
500 ml water
175 g sugar
50 g honey
25 g fresh ginger, finely grated
¾ tbsp salt
½ tsp cinnamon powder
½ tsp garam masala
½ tsp red chilli powder (or less to start and add more later if you would like it spicier)
½ tbsp chaat masala

METHOD

Roughly chop the apricots and place them in a saucepan with the water. Bring to a boil. Add the sugar, honey, ginger, salt, and all the spices. Stir well and let it simmer uncovered for 20–25 minutes, stirring occasionally.

Once thick, glossy and jammy, taste and adjust seasoning if needed (a splash of vinegar or lemon juice can balance the sweetness).

Let the chutney cool before spooning it into a clean jar. The flavours will deepen as it sits.

Blend it smooth or keep it chunky, your call!

STORAGE

Store in the fridge for up to 3 weeks.
Keep in the freezer for up to 3 months.

Mission notes

Switch out the apricots and try it with any other dried fruits.

Want it punchier? Add a splash of vinegar or a few mustard seeds.

CORIANDER & MINT CHUTNEY

This is a staple in our fridge. It's fresh, herby and tangy with just the right amount of heat. It's simple to make – the only thing you need to do is add the ingredients in the correct order. And get yourself a good blender.

धनिया और पुदीने चटनी

INGREDIENTS

10 g oil
2–3 cm ginger, washed and skin scrubbed (no need to peel if the skin is young)
3 cloves of garlic, peeled
1 green chilli (adjust as desired, based on your heat preference or the spiciness of the chilli you have)
½ medium-sized tomato, quartered
1 shallot, peeled and quartered (or ½ red onion)
1 bunch mint, thicker parts of stalk removed (approx. 100 g)
1 bunch coriander (stalks included), roughly chopped (approx. 100 g)
2–3 ice cubes or ice-cold water (will keep the chutney's green colour)
10 g lemon juice (½ lemon)
1 tsp black salt
1 tsp dried mango powder

METHOD

Start by putting the oil at the bottom of your blender; then add the ginger, garlic, green chilli, tomato and shallot. Blitz them to a pulp.

Add the mint and coriander, top with ice and blitz again until you have a smooth paste. Add more ice if needed to achieve your preferred consistency.

Season with lemon juice, black salt and dried mango powder.

STORAGE

Store in the fridge for up to 2 days in an airtight container. The colour might dull, but the flavour will remain.

Store in the freezer for up to 3 months.

Tip:
Use an ice tray to freeze in handy portions.

Mission notes

The balance between the chilli, salt and lemon is key. You can adjust and tailor it to your own taste buds.

Swirl a few spoons through Greek yoghurt or for a plant-based substitute for a cooling dip.

CORIANDER & MINT MAYO

Fresh, creamy, and oh so pleasantly green.

INGREDIENTS

170 g good-quality mayo
40 g coriander and mint chutney (see above)
40 g plain yoghurt (Greek or thick-style)
½ tsp roasted cumin seeds, crushed
1 tsp lime juice
Salt to taste

METHOD

Stir all the ingredients together until green and glossy. Adjust the lime and salt to balance the sharpness and richness. Let it sit in the fridge before serving.

मीठी सौंफ चटनी

SWEET FENNEL CHUTNEY

This is an example of the versatility of tamarind sauce. Combine it with some fennel seeds and some spice, and voila! You have a whole flavour profile. Sweet, spicy and sharp with a hit of fennel, this is tamarind chutney's cooler cousin. It's bold, aromatic, and one of those lesser-known gems that deserves a spot on the table.

INGREDIENTS

100 g fennel seeds
50 g black whole peppercorns
1 tbsp neutral oil (veg or groundnut)
2 tbsp Kashmiri chilli powder (Deggi mirch)
1 l water
500 g sugar
200 ml prepared tamarind chutney (see page 28)

METHOD

Toast the fennel seeds and black peppercorns in a dry pan over medium heat for 1–2 minutes until fragrant. Pound to a coarse powder using a mortar and pestle (or grind in a spice grinder).

Heat the oil in a saucepan. Add the chilli powder and stir quickly – don't let it burn. Immediately pour in the water, bring to a boil, then add the sugar. Stir in the tamarind chutney and let the whole thing simmer gently on low/medium heat for 30–40 minutes, until thick and syrupy.

Add 2 tablespoons of the fennel-pepper powder, stir through and take off the heat.

Let cool completely, then transfer to a clean jar and refrigerate.

Mission notes

Pairs beautifully with fresh or grilled fruits.

Add olive oil and lime or apple cider vinegar for sharpness and you've got instant salad dressing.

You'll have leftover fennel-pepper powder to sprinkle over grilled meat or stir into yoghurt for a punchy dip.

Make sure the pan is hot enough to toast the fennel and pepper, but not so hot that they burn – keep them moving. They should be crispy enough to grind.

STORAGE

Store in the fridge for up to a month (or more). Store in the freezer for up to 3 months.

KARMA KETCHUP
कर्मा केचप

It's ketchup, but for grown-ups. Spicy, sweet, and loaded with bold Sri Lankan flavours like curry leaves, chilli and black mustard seeds. We reach for this whenever regular ketchup just won't cut it.

INGREDIENTS

3 tbsp oil
½ tsp black mustard seeds
1 tbsp minced ginger
2 tbsp minced garlic
20–25 fresh curry leaves
½ green chilli, finely chopped
1 tbsp Kashmiri chilli powder
500 g tomato ketchup
75 g tomato purée
2 tbsp apple cider vinegar
large pinch of salt

Optional extras

½ tsp jaggery or brown sugar
¼ tsp toasted cumin powder
Smoked paprika or chipotle powder
Splash of lime juice at the end

METHOD

Heat the oil in a pan over medium heat. When the oil is warm, add the mustard seeds. Once they start to pop, toss in the ginger, garlic, curry leaves and green chilli. Sauté until the garlic starts turning golden.

Add the chilli powder (and cumin, if using) and stir quickly. Pour in the ketchup, tomato purée, vinegar and jaggery (if using). Bring to a gentle boil, then simmer on low heat for about 10 minutes until thick and glossy. Add salt to taste, and finish with lime juice if you like it punchier. Cool and store in a clean jar.

STORAGE

Store in the fridge for up to a month.

Mission notes

Add a dollop in your curry for a cheeky bit of extra flavour.

Use this like any other ketchup on a burger, hot dog or chips.

CURRY LEAF MAYO

INGREDIENTS
12–15 fresh curry leaves
1 egg yolk
1 tsp Dijon mustard
1 tbsp lemon juice or vinegar
250 ml neutral oil (sunflower or rapeseed)
salt to taste

Optional
1 small garlic clove, grated

METHOD
Toast the curry leaves in a dry pan until crisp. Cool and crush.

In a bowl, whisk the egg yolk, mustard, lemon juice and a pinch of salt. Slowly drizzle in the oil while whisking to form an emulsion (or use a stick blender). Stir in the crushed curry leaves and garlic (if using). Adjust salt and acidity.

CURRY LEAF TARTAR SAUCE

Creamy, herby, crunchy — this isn't your average tartar sauce. We've flipped the script in our version with toasted curry leaves, chaat masala and tangy pickles for a desi twist that works with everything from fried fish to desi masala prawn tacos.

INGREDIENTS
360 g curry leaf mayo (see above)
30 g finely chopped white onion
12 g chopped parsley
50 g finely chopped pickled cucumber
3 g fresh coriander
3 g lime juice (about half a lime)
2 g chunky chaat masala
2 g salt

METHOD
Add all ingredients to a bowl or mixing tub. Stir well until combined – it should be creamy with some texture. Chill before serving.

STORAGE
Store in an airtight container in the fridge for 5–7 days.

Mission notes

Swap pickled cucumber for gherkins, capers or pickled green chillies.

COCONUT SAMBOL

Cool, crunchy, fiery — this no-cook chutney is all about texture and zing. It's our tropical answer to coleslaw: sharp, herby and fresh, with a gentle heat that leaves a coastal aftertaste.

नारियल साम्बोल

INGREDIENTS

½ tsp black peppercorns
½ tsp black mustard seeds (optional)
½ small red onion, finely diced
5 g green chilli, chopped (about 1 small chilli – you can totally adjust this to your own heat tolerance; do keep some in reserve to balance out with the rest of the ingredients)
1 tsp Deggi mirch (Kashmiri chilli powder) or red chilli powder
¼ tsp smoked paprika or hot paprika
100 g fresh coconut, grated (see notes for alternative)
1 tbsp chopped coriander
salt to taste
juice of ½ lime

METHOD

Grind the peppercorns and mustard seeds using a mortar and pestle or spice grinder until coarse. Add the red onion, green chilli, chilli powder and paprika. Pound or mix again to form a rough paste.

Mix in the coconut, coriander, salt and lime juice. Taste and tweak. Add more lime or chilli if you're into it.

Chill before serving, but don't let it sit too long: this sambol is best eaten fresh.

Mission notes

No fresh coconut? Use frozen grated coconut (available in Asian grocery stores). Or soak 100 g of desiccated coconut in 100 ml of hot water for 10 minutes and use as above.

Add 1 tsp of Maldive fish flakes (cured tuna) if you want that traditional umami punch.

Level it up with a quick temper of hot oil, curry leaves and mustard seeds poured over the top.

PICKLED DIAKON
मूली का अचार
PICKLED ONIONS
प्याज का आचार
PICKLED CUCUMBER
खीरे का आचार

ACID DROPS / SHARP CORNERS
PICKLES

Sharp, quick and essential. Pickling might be having its moment, but for us, it's always been a necessity. At Mission, pickles aren't just on the side – they're part of the system. They cut through the richness, reset your palate, and bring that extra snap to every bite.

We keep our method simple on purpose:

1. The brine stays sharp and bold so it doesn't get lost in all the other flavours on the plate.

2. You've already put effort into the rest of the meal, this bit should be easy.

Plus, the colours don't hurt. Luminous pink onions, solar yellow turmeric roots, ruby chillies. They don't just taste good; they make your table look good too.

NORTH INDIAN PICKLING LIQUID

Sweet, spiced and sharp. This style is often used for pickled onions, daikon or pineapple served with chaats or BBQ. It's vinegar-based, but softened with sugar and warm spices.

INGREDIENTS **makes 1 litre**

750 ml apple cider vinegar (5%)
250 ml water
600 g sugar
2 bay leaves
3 star anise
1 tsp yellow mustard seeds
½ tsp crushed black pepper
1 small stick of cinnamon (optional)
2 cloves (optional)

METHOD

Add all the ingredients to a saucepan and bring to a boil. Simmer for 5–7 minutes until the sugar dissolves and the spices release their aroma.

Cool completely.

Pick your vegetables, slice finely and cover with the liquid. Store overnight in an airtight container to allow the juices to combine and to bring the pickles to life.

PICK YOUR FRUIT OR VEG

Sliced red onions – add a few chunks of beetroot for the bright colour.

Peeled and sliced mooli (daikon) – add a pinch of turmeric powder.

Pineapple – chop some green chillies into the pickle for a flavour bomb.

Cucumber slices – salt the slices before pickling to release the water from the cucumbers. Dab the salt off with kitchen paper and add a pinch of turmeric.

SOUTH INDIAN PICKLING LIQUID

Tangy, slightly spiced and fragrant. This one's lighter on sugar, and finished with a tempered oil for aroma. Works well with vegetables like carrots, green mango or chillies.

INGREDIENTS **makes 1 litre**

700 ml apple cider vinegar (5%)
300 ml water
200 g sugar (or jaggery)
1½ tsp salt
1 tbsp neutral oil (for tempering)
1 tsp mustard seeds
½ tsp fenugreek seeds
2 dried red chillies
a few fresh curry leaves

METHOD

In a pot, bring vinegar, water, sugar and salt to a gentle boil. Simmer for 3–4 minutes.

In a separate pan, heat the oil. Add the mustard seeds, fenugreek, dried chillies and curry leaves. Let the spices crackle for 30 seconds.

Pour the tempered oil into the brine. Stir and cool completely.

Pick your vegetables, slice finely and cover with the liquid. Store overnight in an airtight container to allow the juices to combine and to bring the pickles to life.

PICK YOUR FRUIT OR VEG

Green mango – slice thin or julienne, add a pinch of chilli powder for bite.

Green beans – lightly blanch before pickling to keep the crunch.

Carrot batons – pair with curry leaves and a few mustard seeds for that classic taste.

Fresh ginger – thinly sliced, makes a sharp and fragrant sidekick to any rice dish.

Shaved red cabbage – not traditional, but takes on the tempering beautifully and adds great crunch to dosas or rice.

BREAKFAST

ब्रेकफास्ट

WAKEY WAKEY, EGGS AND MASALA.

Indian breakfasts were always a thing in our house. Served with a warm chai (or *chaa* as we call it), to wash down the fattiness.

Here you'll find our take on the AM classics — spicy omelettes, buttery stuffed parathas and bacon with a tamarind twist. These dishes are perfectly hearty for a lazy weekend meal or to cure a hangover. Masala mornings are the best mornings.

ब्रेकफास्ट परथस
BREAKFAST PARATHAS

I grew up in a Punjabi household where parathas were only round when stuffed, and square when folded with butter and layered with love. They still come off the tawa golden, dripping in butter and crispy at the edges, the kind you tear into with your hands and mop up with full-fat yoghurt or raita and a pinch of achaar.

We use atta, a finely milled whole wheat flour that's softer and more finely ground than Western wholemeal. It gives parathas their signature chew while keeping things light and pliable, perfect for folding and layering.

THREE WAYS TO PARATHA

1
PLAIN PARATHA
पलाइन पराठा

Classic, square, with just butter, salt and a pinch of paratha masala folded in.

2
MIXED MASALA PARATHA
मेथी पराठा

Spices, herbs and flavour are built straight into the dough. These can be made with fresh ingredients like chopped methi (fenugreek) leaves, coriander, onions or grated garlic, or with leftovers like day-old dal kneaded in. Bold, messy, and full of texture.

3
STUFFED PARATHA
आलू पराठा

The OG paratha. Filled with spiced potatoes, grated and spiced cauliflower, seasoned paneer, leftover keema or anything you've got on hand. They're hearty, hands-on, and proper soul food.

पलाइन पराठा
1. PLAIN PARATHA

Folding traps the ghee inside, giving you crispy layers, a perfect bite and flakiness in all the right places. This is the ultimate North Indian flatbread.

INGREDIENTS **makes 8 parathas**

350 g whole wheat flour (atta), plus more for dusting
260 ml water
melted ghee or butter
paratha masala (see page 45)

METHOD

Tip the flour into a mixing bowl and slowly pour in the water, mixing with your fingers until it just comes together. Knead lightly for a minute or so – no need to go full power here. Let it rest under a tea towel for 10 minutes.

Now give it a proper knead for 2–3 minutes until it's smooth, stretchy and a little tacky. Cover and let rest in the fridge.

Take the dough out and divide into 8 roughly equal portions (about 100 g each). Roll into balls, dust with flour and flatten into a small round, about the size of your palm.

1. Roll out your dough to a circle about 10 cm across and add a teaspoon of butter in the centre, spread slightly and add a sprinkle of paratha masala.
2. Fold the top edge down, then the bottom up to overlap slightly.
3. Fold the left side in, then the right, to create a rough square.
4. Press gently to seal, dust with flour and roll out again into a bigger square (about 20 cm).

Heat a pan on medium. Roll each dough square out into a larger square, around 20 cm across. Drop it on the hot pan. Once you see faint brown spots (30–60 seconds), flip it.

Brush the top with ghee or oil, flip again, and do the same on the other side. Keep flipping until golden, flaky, and maybe a little puffed.

SCAN TO SEE HOW IT'S DONE

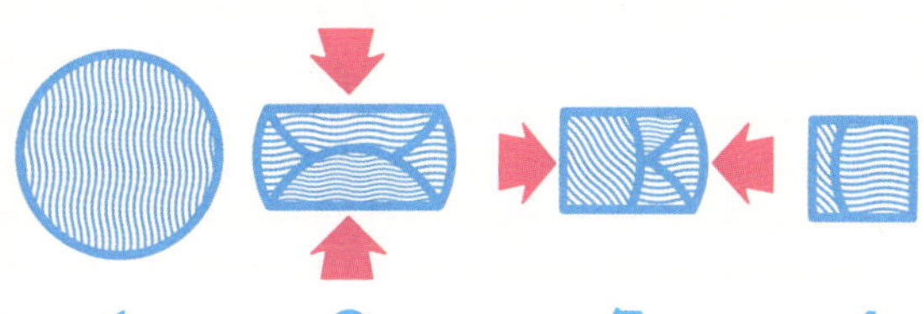

मेथी पराठा

2. MIXED MASALA PARATHA

A herby upgrade to the classic. Fresh methi, fiery green chillies, and masala folded right into the dough. These are your go-to when you want all the flavour without the filling stress

INGREDIENTS **makes 8 parathas**

290 g atta (whole wheat flour), plus extra for rolling
1 tsp salt
½ tsp turmeric
1 tsp garam masala
180 g fresh methi (fenugreek), washed, dried and chopped.
3–4 green finger chillies, finely chopped
225 ml cool water (adjust as needed)
melted ghee or butter

METHOD

In a mixing bowl, combine atta with salt, turmeric and garam masala. Add your chopped methi and chillies. Gradually add water, kneading into a soft, slightly sticky dough. Cover and rest for 30–60 minutes, in the fridge.

Divide into 8 balls and roll each one out into a small round. Brush with melted ghee, fold edges in to make a square and let them rest for a few more minutes.

Roll each square out again into a larger square (around 15 cm). Cook on a hot tawa until you see golden spots and bubbles, then flip, brush with ghee and cook both sides until crispy and puffed.

Mission notes

No methi? Dill, spinach or mustard leaves work just as well.

Got leftover dhal or saag? Add a few spoonfuls into the dough for bonus flavour.

3. STUFFED PARATHA

आलू पराठा

Golden, flaky and stuffed with spicy mashed potato, this is North Indian comfort food at its best. My #1 paratha.

INGREDIENTS **makes 8 parathas**

For the dough
350 g atta (whole wheat flour), plus extra for rolling
260 ml water

For the filling
180 g potatoes
1 small onion grated (squeeze out all the liquid using your hands or a clean cloth, don't skip this).
2–3 green chillies, finely chopped (adjust to heat)
½ tsp cumin seeds
½ tsp garam masala
½ tsp salt
a small handful of fresh coriander, chopped

For cooking
melted ghee, butter or oil

METHOD

Dough

Mix the atta gradually with water and knead until soft. Let rest for 15 minutes. Knead again for a couple of minutes and cover. Chill in the fridge for about an hour – this will make it easier to handle later. This recipe should give you a firm dough. If by any chance you ended up with dough that's too sticky to roll, you can knead again and add some extra flour or chill the dough a bit longer.

The filling

Boil and mash the potatoes until smooth. Add the onion, ginger, chillies, cumin, garam masala, salt and coriander. Mix well and taste. Mash the potatoes while still warm so they will mix with the spices better.

Shape and stuff

Divide the dough into 8 balls. Roll each into a small disc and spoon in some filling. Pinch to seal each paratha and shape into a smooth ball again.

Roll and cook

Dust the parathas with flour and gently roll each one into a flat disc (about 17–18 cm). Place on a hot tawa or pan. Cook until bubbles form, then flip. Brush with ghee, flip again and let both sides go golden and crisp.

Mission notes

For a level-up, add ajwain (carom seeds) or kasuri methi to the dough.

मां 'स पराठा मसाला

This is my mum's go-to finishing move. This roasted spice blend adds instant zing to pretty much anything: a buttery paratha, a bowl of yoghurt or even your next lassi. Tangy, earthy, salty and punchy, it's like chaat masala's cooler cousin.

INGREDIENTS **makes 140 g**

50 g cumin seeds (jeera)
50 g dry coriander seeds
10 g red chilli flakes (adjust to taste)
15 g pink salt
15 g black salt

METHOD

Toast the cumin seeds in a dry pan on medium heat until fragrant (about a minute). Let them cool.

Combine the coriander seeds, roasted cumin, chilli flakes, pink salt and black salt.

Grind to your preferred texture: coarse for a bit of crunch, fine if you want it smooth and dusty.

Store in an airtight jar.

USE IT

Stirred into yoghurt or churned into lassi. As a finishing touch on parathas or chaats. Even a secret seasoning for popcorn or chips (trust us).

Mission notes

For a smoky twist, toast the coriander seeds too.

You can swap red chilli flakes for Kashmiri chilli powder if you want it less textured.

Add a pinch of dry mango powder (amchur) if you like extra tang.

TIPS FROM THE TAWA

Rest your dough: Let it sit for 15 minutes once kneaded. This makes rolling easier and keeps the parathas soft.

Prep the dough balls: Rolling and folding the parathas all at once before you start rolling them out and putting them on the pan will make the whole process a lot less stressful.

Always melt your ghee or butter before brushing as it's way easier to handle and spreads more evenly.

Tawa: Use a traditional tawa or a non-stick frying pan or pancake pan. Cook over medium heat for a steady, even cook.

Watch the heat: Let the paratha bubble and brown before flipping. Don't be afraid to give it some time on the pan.

Serve right: With cold yoghurt, spicy achaar and if you want to do it right, a cup of chai.

RAITA
रायता

Whip this up while your parathas are cooking. It's cooling, creamy and takes the edge off that paratha masala.

INGREDIENTS **serves 4**

200 g full-fat yoghurt
½ cucumber, grated and water squeezed out
½ tsp roasted cumin seeds, crushed
pinch of black salt
pinch of amchur
chopped fresh coriander
Optional: a dash of lime juice or chilli powder

METHOD

Mix all the ingredients together and chill. Spoon it next to your hot paratha and dive in.

कैसे करें : आलू पराठा
HOW TO: STUFFED ALOO PARATHA

PREPARE THE DOUGH AND FILLING

(see recipes on page 44)

1.
Use the pads of four fingers to push down into the centre of the dough ball, spreading it into a small, even disc. Leave the outer rim slightly thicker than the centre so the filling has a lip to sit in.

2.
Turn the disc over and dust both sides with a little flour to stop it sticking. Tap off any excess so you're not adding too much.

3.
Cup the dough with both hands and gently roll/press it between your palms, widening it into a flat round.

4.
Lightly flour the surface and roll the disc out until it's 10 cm wide. Rotate the dough as you roll so the thickness stays even; don't roll paper-thin at this stage.

5.
Spoon a heaped tablespoon of cooled potato mixture into the middle, keeping the filling mound low and centred. Overfilling is the main cause of leaks later.

6.
Bring the rim in towards the filling, folding small sections over and slightly overlapping as you go until the entire filling is enclosed. Think of gathering a small pouch rather than one big fold.

7.
Press down on the top of the parcel with the heel of your hand, checking that all the folds are sealed well and there are no gaps. Once sealed, dust lightly with flour so it won't stick when you roll again.

8.
Using light, even strokes, roll the parcel out from the centre. Turn it frequently and re-dust under and over with a little flour if the filling shows through or the dough sticks. If a seam opens, press and pinch it closed, then continue.

Roll the paratha into an even, thin round. Press down on the top of the parcel with the heel of your hand, checking that all the folds are sealed well and there are no gaps.

9.
The surface should be smooth and the stuffing fully enclosed. Transfer gently to the hot pan for cooking.

SCAN TO SEE HOW IT'S DONE

Quick tips:

Keep the flour sparing – too much makes the paratha dry.

If the stuffing peeks out while rolling, stop, reseal and dust before continuing.

Turn the dough as you roll for an even, circular paratha.

एग भुर्जी

EGG BHURJI

INDIAN SCRAMBLED EGGS

serves 2

Fluffy, spicy, slightly greasy. India's answer to the breakfast burrito filling.

INGREDIENTS

2 tbsp oil or ghee
1 tsp cumin seeds
1 small onion, chopped
½ tomato, chopped
1 tsp green chilli, minced
½ tsp turmeric
½ tsp salt
½ tsp garam masala
6 large eggs (whisked)
knob of butter (optional but highly recommended)
1 tbsp chopped coriander

METHOD

Heat oil in a pan and fry the cumin seeds until they pop. Add the onion and fry until lightly browned. Add the tomato and cook until it is fried well. Add chilli, turmeric and salt. Fry for a few minutes. Add garam masala and gently stir in the eggs until scrambled. Turn the heat off, stir in the knob of butter and garnish with the coriander.

Mission notes

Serve with buttered toast or wrapped in a roti.

Add cheese or a dollop of pickle on the side.

मसाला आमलेट
MASALA OMELETTE

serves 2

Simple on the spice, soft on the inside. No-nonsense brunch hero.

INGREDIENTS
4 eggs (medium-sized)
salt and pepper
2 tbsp onion, finely chopped
1/2 tomato, finely chopped
1 tsp green chilli, minced
1 tbsp chopped coriander
½ tsp roasted cumin seeds
oil or butter (as much as your pan needs for an omelette)
pinch of chilli powder
pinch of chaat masala

METHOD

Beat the eggs with salt, pepper, dry spices, tomato, onion, coriander and chilli. Fry in hot oil or butter until golden on the outside and soft on the inside. Serve folded or open style.

Mission notes

Top with grated cheese of your choice. Eat folded inside a naan with our tamarind bacon (see page 52) and karma ketchup (see page 33) or as a DIY brekkie wrap.

For a healthier option, load with baby spinach or avocado. Pairs perfectly with toast and pickles.

टामारिंड बेकन

makes 4 portions **TAMARIND BACON**

Sweet, sticky, tangy and a very good reason to get out of bed.

INGREDIENTS
200 ml tamarind chutney (see page 28)
50 g brown sugar
½ tsp chilli flakes
cracked black pepper
1 cinnamon stick
3 pcs star anise
12 rashers of streaky bacon

Optional to add to the glaze
½ tsp grated ginger
½ tsp grated garlic

METHOD

Combine all ingredients except for the bacon in a pan and simmer on medium heat until the consistency becomes thicker, like a sticky syrup. Brush the tamarind glaze over the bacon.

Heat oven to 160°C.

Place bacon evenly spread on an oven tray lined with baking paper. Place tray in the middle of the oven. Flip the bacon over after 10–12 minutes and cook until you have your desired texture, crispy or tender. You can adjust the cooking time depending on the thickness and fattiness of your bacon.

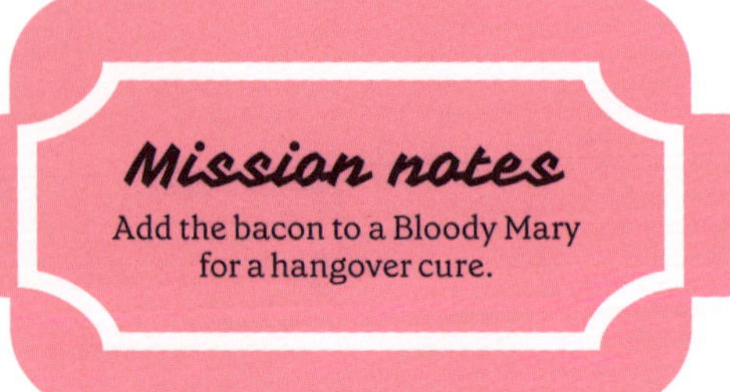

DESI DALIYA
INDIAN PORRIDGE

serves 4

Rich, creamy, sweet and a very good reason to get out of bed. The warmth and aroma of this porridge, along with the steady fuel it gives you for the day, make it a dish with real staying power. It's a winning winter classic in our house.

INGREDIENTS

2 tbsp ghee, coconut oil or butter
120 g rolled oats
500 ml whole milk (or use almond/coconut milk)
½ tsp ground cardamom
¼ tsp cinnamon
pinch of Himalayan pink salt
2 tbsp jaggery or brown sugar (adjust to taste)
1–2 tbsp chopped dates or raisins
1 tbsp chopped cashews or almonds (toasted)

To top

Fresh seasonal fruit & seeds of your choice

Optional

pinch of saffron, dash of rosewater

METHOD

In a saucepan, heat the ghee. Toast the oats gently for 1–2 minutes until nutty. Add the milk and bring to a gentle simmer. Stir in the cardamom, cinnamon and salt. Let it simmer for 5–7 minutes, stirring occasionally, until thick and creamy.

Add the jaggery (or sugar) and the dates or raisins, and continue to cook until fully melted in. If using saffron, add it now.

Once it's thick and pudding-like, remove from the heat. Finish with toasted nuts and a tiny splash of rosewater if you're feeling fancy.

Mission notes

Want it richer? Stir in a splash of condensed milk, a spoonful of almond butter or tahini.

Make it vegan with coconut milk and to go full coconut, substitute coconut sugar for the jaggery as well.

EAT

INDIA
भारत
मिनी

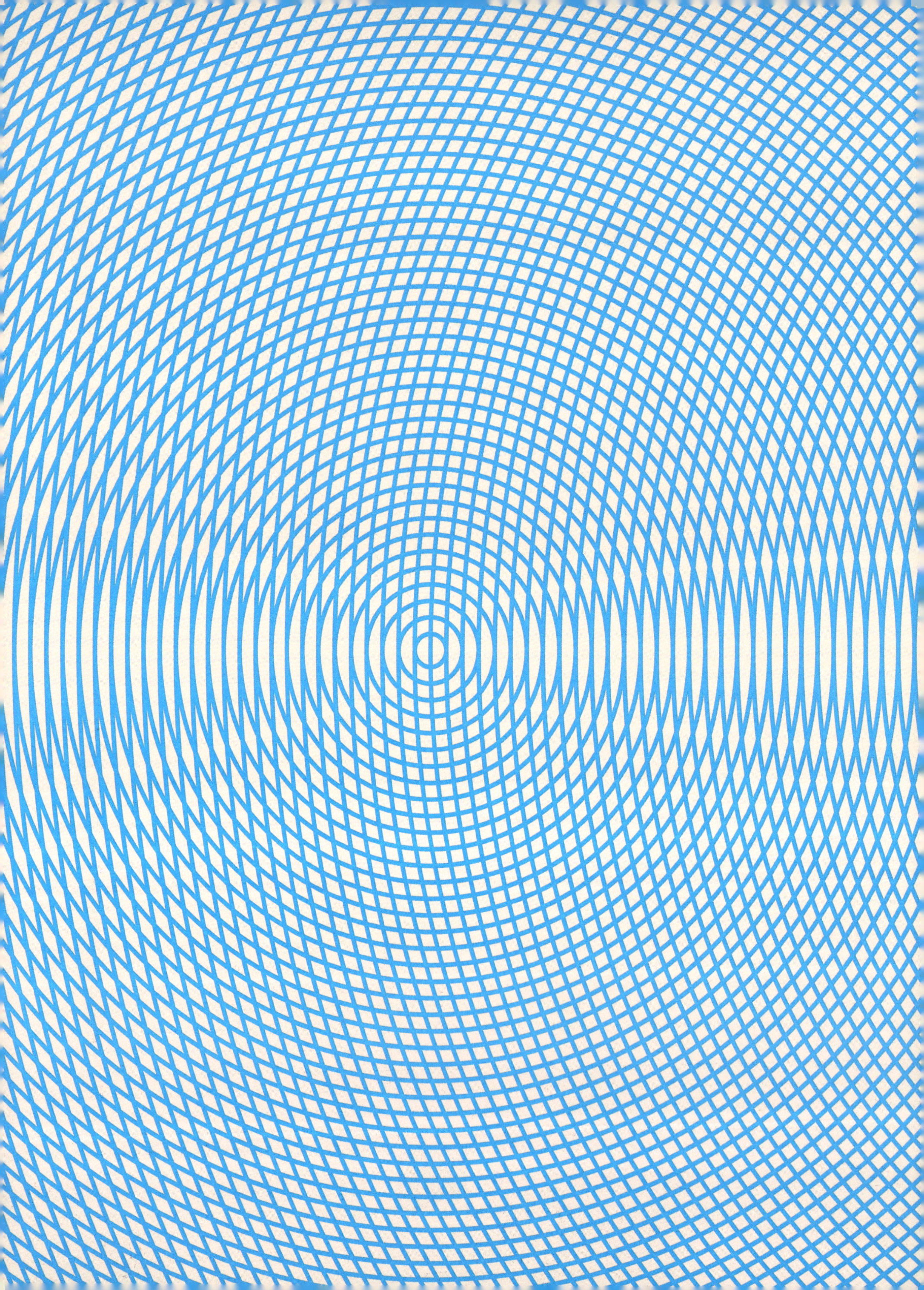

SNACKS

शेयरिंग स्नैक्स

BITE-SIZED CHAOS.

Snacks are our love language. From street-side samosas to anything deep-fried, sauced-up or loaded with toppings – these are the little dishes that start the party (and more often than not, are the party).

At Mission Masala, we think everything tastes better when it's shared – and snacks are the best way to do that. Whether you're serving them as starters or sides, or just throwing a few extras on the table for a proper feast, this is the section that brings the goodies.

समोसा
SAMOSAS

makes 15–16 samosas

The secret to a proper samosa isn't just the filling, but the dough. Good samosa pastry should be firm enough to hold its shape, easy to roll thin, and fry up golden and crisp without going greasy. The trick is binding the flour with oil and just enough water to make a smooth, pliable dough. Rest it, roll it and you've got the perfect casing for anything you want to fill them with.

INGREDIENTS
For the dough
1 kg plain flour
150 ml sunflower oil
20 g salt
16 g lemon juice
1½ g baking powder
375 ml water

METHOD

Combine the flour, oil, salt, lemon juice and baking powder in a large bowl. Rub the oil into the flour with your fingertips until it resembles breadcrumbs.

Gradually add water, a little at a time, and knead until you have a smooth, firm dough.

Cover with a damp cloth and let it rest for 20–30 minutes before rolling.

Once the dough has rested, divide it into 60 g balls ready for shaping.

Mission notes

Make the samosas in bigger batches, half-fry to prevent sticking and freeze in an airtight container.

When ready to eat, let them thaw slightly before deep-frying for perfect crispness.

Storage tip
Freeze in an airtight container for up to a month. For best results, fry fresh or from a semi-thawed state.

1. CLASSIC POTATO & PEA FILLING

Soft, spiced and comforting, this is the filling everyone knows and loves. Hearty potatoes, sweet peas and a perfect balance of spices.

INGREDIENTS
500 g potatoes, peeled
20 g salt
1 tsp crushed red chilli flakes
2 tsp chilli powder
2 tsp cumin seeds
1 tsp coriander powder
½ tsp dried fenugreek leaves (methi)
75 g frozen peas

METHOD

Cut the potatoes into 3–4 cm chunks and boil them in salted water until just tender and cooked through but still holding their shape. Drain well, then crush lightly with a spoon or masher to a coarse texture (not a purée).

Stir in the fresh and dry spices until evenly mixed. Finally, fold in the frozen peas gently (no need to defrost them first).

2. TAMARIND OYSTER MUSHROOM FILLING

A great meaty alternative that's full of umami, tang and spice. Roasted pulled oyster mushrooms tossed in our versatile tamarind sauce create a sticky, flavour-packed filling. Perfect for adventurous samosas — the sky's the limit when it comes to experimenting with fillings.

INGREDIENTS

- 1.2 kg oyster mushrooms, pulled into strips (yields ~700 g cooked)
- 30 ml oil
- 15 g salt
- 1 tsp coarse black pepper
- 120 ml tamarind sauce (see page 28)
- 10 g brown sugar (2 tsp)
- 2 tsp chilli powder
- 2 tsp cumin seeds
- 20 g garlic, minced
- 120 g red onion, finely chopped
- 20 g fresh coriander, chopped

METHOD

Preheat oven to 180°C. Spread the pulled mushrooms on a tray, drizzle with oil, season with salt and pepper, and roast for 10 minutes until they shrink down and some of the moisture is gone (should yield about 700 g cooked).

Warm the tamarind sauce in a small pan with brown sugar and chilli powder until glossy.

Heat a little oil in a pan, fry cumin seeds until they crackle, then add garlic and onion. Cook until softened and golden. Add the roasted mushrooms, stir to coat, then pour in the tamarind sauce. Cook together for a few minutes until the mushrooms are sticky and well-coated.

Remove from the heat and add chopped coriander. Let cool before filling the samosas (about 65 g each).

3. CHEESEBURGER FILLING

Bold, indulgent and fun. Think juicy, spiced beef or lamb with melted cheddar, finished with fresh coriander. Serve with mustard, karma ketchup (page 33) and pickled cucumbers (page 37) for a street food-style samosa that's full of mischief and flavour.

INGREDIENTS

- 500 g beef (chuck roll, coarsely ground)
- 450 g cheddar, grated
- 145 g red onion, finely chopped
- 30 g garlic, minced
- 27 g fresh coriander, chopped
- 22 g toasted coriander seeds (3½ tbsp)
- 16 g mustard seeds (1¾ tbsp)
- 11 g red chilli flakes (2 tsp)
- 32 g salt (1¾ tbsp)
- 13 g coarse black pepper (2 tsp)
- 27 g mustard (1½ tbsp)

METHOD

Combine all the ingredients in a large bowl. Mix thoroughly until the beef, cheese, spices and aromatics are evenly distributed.

The filling is now ready to portion into samosas (about 65 g per samosa).

Cover and refrigerate until you are ready to fill the samosas.

1.

2.

3.

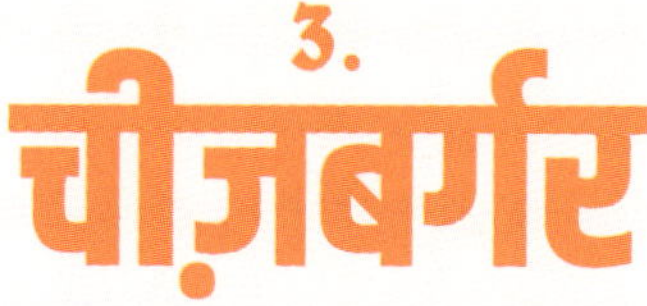

कैसे करें
HOW TO: SAMOSA
समोसा

roll → pocket → fill → seal

SCAN TO SEE
HOW IT'S DONE

MAKE THE SEALING SLURRY

Mix 2 tbsp plain flour (maida) with 3–4 tbsp water into a thick, paintable paste (no lumps).

ROLL THE SHEET

1.
Lightly dust the work surface. Flatten a dough ball (about 25–30 g) into a puck.

2.
Roll into an oval about 15–18 cm long and 2 mm thick – aim for even edges.

3.
Cut through the narrow width (the short side) to make two long half-ovals.

4.
Keep them covered with a damp cloth so they don't dry out.

MAKE THE POCKET

5.
Take one half-oval with the straight cut side facing up. Use your index finger to hold the sheet halfway down the edge and let the top half hang.

6.
Brush a thin line of slurry along the entire straight edge resting on your finger.

7.
Form a cone by bringing the two ends of the straight edge together with a 1 cm overlap; press to seal the seam.

8.
Important: pinch both corners at the top and bottom of the seam so the cone is watertight. Run a finger over the seam to compress and smooth.

FILL

9.
Hold the cone in your palm and fold the edges over your index finger and thumb. Spoon in 1½–2 tbsp (60g) filling (don't overfill).

Use your thumb to gently pack the filling down so there's headroom to close.

SEAL THE MOUTH

10.
Brush slurry all around the open mouth (rim) of the cone.

11.
Close: bring the front lip to the back lip, align the edges and pinch to seal from one corner to the other. Lock the corners: press each corner firmly so there are no gaps. Then crimp or press along the entire mouth and the side seam once more.

12.
Check every samosa: make sure there are no visible cracks, corners are firmly pinched and seams are smooth. Place samosas seam-side down on a dusted tray; keep covered with a damp cloth while you shape the rest. Don't let them touch until they meet in the fryer, otherwise they will stick.

If a crack appears, dab with slurry, press and let sit 2–3 minutes before frying.

Fry on low/medium heat first (so the crust sets), then raise the heat to colour.

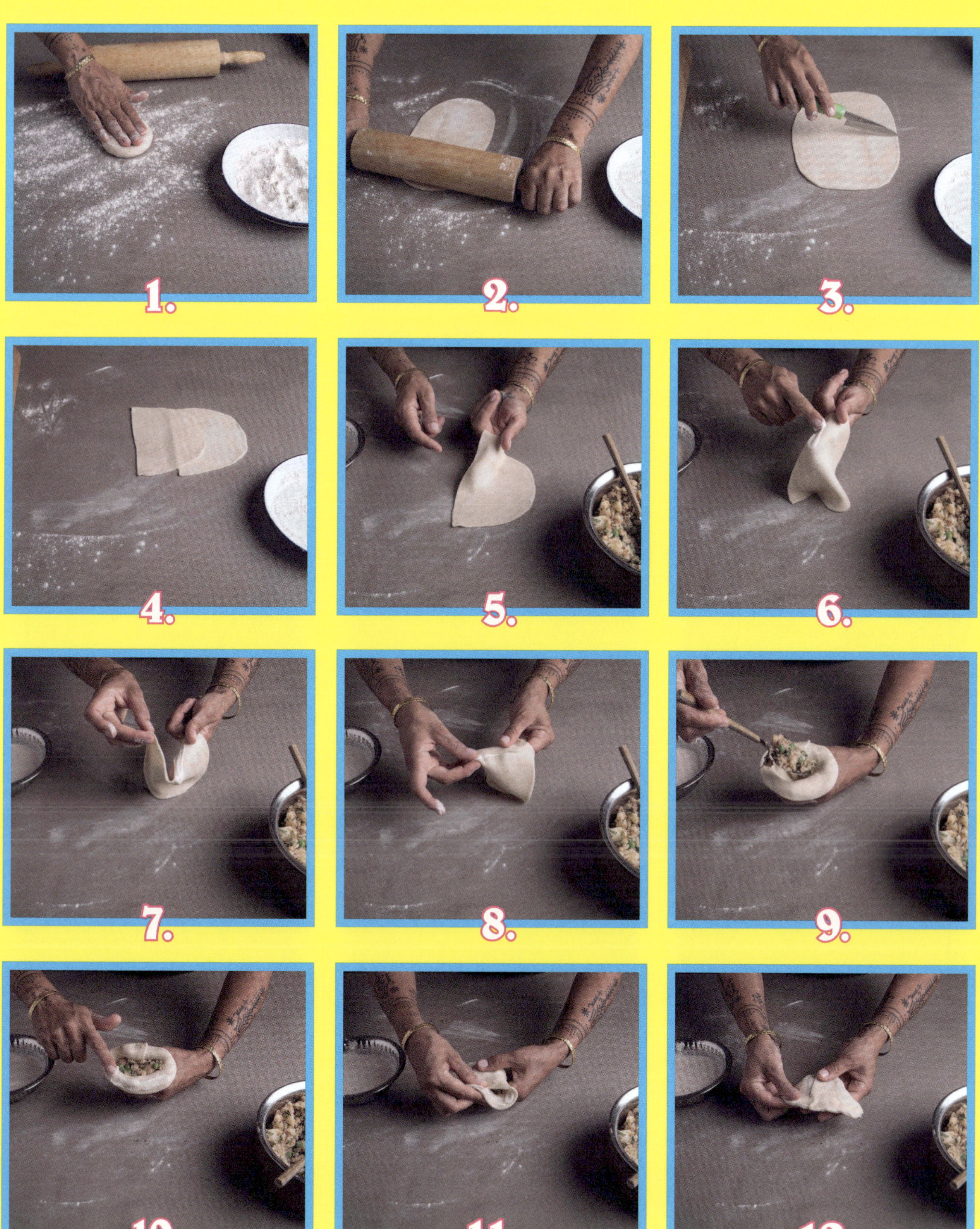
1.
2.
3.
4.
5.
6.
7.
8.
9.
10.
11.
12.

बैंग बैंग भाजी

makes 8–10 servings

BANG BANG BHAJIS

Crispy, golden and packed with seasonal vegetables, these bhajis are perfect all year round. Enjoy them as a snack with sweet mango lassi, warm chai, or tucked into a wrap with salad for a midweek dinner. You can mix and match vegetables; kale, pumpkin, sweet potato, cauliflower, or whatever you like. These bhajis are lactose-free and gluten-free, making them suitable for most dietary requirements.

INGREDIENTS

For the fresh veg & herb mix

250 g finely sliced onions
15 g chopped coriander
50 g chopped spinach leaves (including stalks)
100 g chopped cauliflower, 2–3 cm pieces
100 g finely sliced potato, 2–3 cm pieces

For the batter mix

300 g gram flour (chickpea flour)
400 ml ice-cold water, sparkling water or your favourite beer
3 g coriander seeds
3 g ajwain (lovage seeds)
5 g cumin seeds
1 g dried fenugreek (pinch)
2 g turmeric powder
½ tsp asafoetida powder
1 tsp garam masala
5 g Deggi chilli powder (or alternative chilli powder)
15 g salt

METHOD

Chop and slice all vegetables and herbs, then set aside.

In a bowl, combine the dry batter ingredients and whole spices. Gradually add water while whisking until the batter is thick and smooth. Pour the batter over the vegetables and use your hands to mix until everything is fully coated.

Heat oil in a deep fryer or heavy pan. Test the temperature with a slice of onion; it should sizzle gently. Portion small balls of the bhaji mixture using a tablespoon or ice cream scoop. Fry until golden brown and cooked through, turning occasionally.

Serve immediately with sweet apricot chutney (page 30) and spicy mint and coriander chutney (page 31).

SCAN TO SEE HOW IT'S DONE

Mission notes

When choosing your own vegetables, the total amount should never exceed the quantity of onions. Vegetables with high water content, such as courgette or aubergine, can reduce crispiness.

MDH
CHUNKY CHAT MASALA
Net Wt. / Poids net 100 g

क्रिस्पी केल चाट
CRISPY KALE CHAAT

serves 4

A light, crunchy and spiced kale snack that's perfect for midweek munching or a fun starter. Using the same flavourful bhaji batter, the kale turns crisp while keeping a touch of bite, then gets dressed in tangy chaat flavours for a punchy street food-style treat.

INGREDIENTS

For the kale & herb mix

6–8 whole kale leaves, depending on size.
10 g fresh coriander, chopped

Optional

1 small green chilli, finely chopped

For the batter mix (from Bang Bang Bhajis, see page 66)

150 g gram flour (chickpea flour)
200 ml ice-cold water, sparkling water or beer
2 g coriander seeds
2 g ajwain (lovage seeds)
3 g cumin seeds
1 g dried fenugreek (pinch)
1 g turmeric powder
½ tsp asafoetida powder
3 g Deggi chilli powder (or alternative)
7 g salt

For the chaat dressing

2 tbsp tamarind chutney (see page 28)
2 tbsp coriander & mint chutney (see page 31)
1 tbsp sweet yoghurt (mix in sugar to make it sweet)
1 tsp chaat masala
fresh coriander, chopped, to garnish
1 tbsp pomegranate seeds
1 tbsp finely chopped red onions
sev or crushed papdi for topping (optional)

METHOD

Wash the kale leaves (don't tear) and pat dry. Trim down the stalks of the kale leaves. Keep a long enough end to hold and dip into the batter. Set aside.

In a bowl, combine the batter ingredients and whisk with water until smooth and thick.

Heat oil in a deep pan or fryer. Test with a small piece of leaf; it should sizzle gently.

Take a leaf by its stalk and dip it completely in the batter. Make sure it is fully coated.

Fry the kale leaf by leaf until crisp and lightly golden on both sides, about 2–3 minutes. Drain on paper towels.

Place the fried kale on a plate, dust with chaat masala, drizzle with all 3 sauces and garnish with chopped onions, coriander, pomegranate seeds and sev or crushed papdi if desired. Serve immediately.

चिकन मोमो

makes 70 momos

CHICKEN MOMOS

Nepal and India share a rich culinary heritage, especially in the Himalayan and northern regions. Many of the flavours, techniques and spices overlap, from cumin, coriander and turmeric to ginger, garlic and fresh herbs. Nepali momos are essentially dumplings, a form of street food that resonates deeply with Indian snack traditions. A juicy chicken filling spiced with momo masala, coriander and spring onions, lifted with a sizzling hot oil pour infused with cumin and fenugreek. Wrapped in soft dough and steamed, these momos are a true flavour bomb and that's why they snuck their way in here.

INGREDIENTS

For the dough

500 g all-purpose flour
1 tsp salt
230 ml water

For the filling

1 kg minced chicken (thigh meat preferred)
500 g red onion, finely diced
2 green chillies, finely chopped
2 tbsp ginger-garlic paste
50 g momo masala (see recipe opposite)
50 g fresh coriander, finely chopped
1 pack spring onions, thinly sliced

For the hot oil seasoning

200 g neutral oil
1 tbsp fenugreek seeds
1 tsp cumin seeds
1 tsp coriander powder
1 tsp turmeric
1 tsp garam masala

METHOD

Make the dough by combining the flour, salt and water until you have a smooth, soft dough. Knead well, then cover and rest in the fridge for an hour before rolling.

For the filling, add the onion, green chilli, coriander and spring onion to a large bowl. Spread the minced chicken over the top, then add the ginger-garlic paste and momo masala.

Heat the oil in a pan and add the fenugreek seeds and cumin seeds. Fry until fragrant, then take off the heat and stir in the coriander powder, turmeric and garam masala.

Pour the hot spiced oil straight over the chicken mixture. Mix everything by hand until the filling becomes sticky and well-bound.

Roll out the dough into small wrappers. Place about 20 g of filling in each wrapper, fold and pleat tightly.

Steam the momos until the dough is tender and the chicken is fully cooked, about 8–10 minutes.

HOMEMADE MOMO MASALA

INGREDIENTS **makes ~½ cup**

1 tbsp green cardamom pods, seeds removed
1 tsp black cardamom seeds (about 3 pods)
1 tsp mace (or pinch of nutmeg)
2 tsp cinnamon powder (or 1 small stick)
2 tsp black peppercorns
1 tsp cloves
2 bay leaves
1 tbsp fennel seeds
1 tbsp cumin seeds
1 tbsp coriander seeds
1 tsp turmeric powder
1 tbsp dry ginger powder
1 tbsp garlic powder (or granulated garlic)
1 tbsp onion powder
1 tsp star anise (about 1 pod)
1–2 tsp salt (optional)

METHOD

Toast the whole spices gently in a dry pan until fragrant, making sure not to burn them. Cool completely before grinding to a fine powder. Mix in the turmeric, ginger, garlic, onion powder and salt, then store in an airtight jar in a cool, dry place.

कैसे करें : समोसा
HOW TO: MOMOS

1.
Start with a smooth ball of kneaded dough.

2.
Lightly flour the surface and roll out the dough evenly.

3.
Roll into a large, thin sheet.

4.
Use a cutter (about 7–8 cm in diameter) to stamp out circles of dough.

5.
Lift out the momo wrappers and repeat the process with the remaining dough.

6.
Place one wrapper in your palm and spoon about 1 tablespoon of filling into the centre.

7.
Pinch one side of the wrapper closed to secure the filling.

8.
Hold the half-sealed momo in your left hand, with the filling tucked in.
Use your left thumb to gently press the filling down so it stays compact.

With your right hand, start pleating from one side: fold a small section of dough over and pinch it against the back edge to seal.

Keep moving along the edge, folding and pinching each pleat over to the right, while your left hand keeps the momo steady.

9.
Work your way across until you reach the other end. The pleats should curve naturally, creating that classic crescent shape.

मशरूम 65

serves 6
(snack/starter)

MUSHROOM 65

Crispy, spicy oyster mushrooms with a punch of South Indian flavour. Perfect as a starter or a snack and great with curry leaf mayo, these are always a hit on any table! Traditionally these are made with chicken, but the seasoned batter lends itself to anything.

INGREDIENTS

For the marinade

550 g oyster mushrooms
100 ml yoghurt
30 ml lime juice
1 tbsp Deggi mirch
70 g ginger-garlic paste
2 tsp crushed black pepper
1 tsp salt (or to taste)

For the batter

120 g TRS rice flour
80 g cornflour
2 tsp Deggi mirch
2 tsp coriander powder
1 tsp turmeric powder
1 tsp chaat masala
120–160 ml water

For the garnish

20 curry leaves, fried
amchur (mango powder) to dust

METHOD

Tear the mushrooms apart with your hands into medium-sized strips.

Combine all the ingredients for the marinade and coat the mushrooms evenly. Don't let the mushrooms sit for too long because they will release their water, which could give them a spongy texture when fried.

In a separate bowl, combine all the batter ingredients except the water. Add water gradually while beating until you have a thick smooth batter that will stick to the mushrooms.

Dip the marinated mushrooms in the batter and coat them well.

In a deep pan or fryer, heat the oil to 170–180°C. Flash-fry the curry leaves and set aside.

Fry the mushrooms in batches until crisp and golden.

Drain on paper towels, dust with amchur powder and garnish with crispy curry leaves. Serve immediately with curry leaf mayo (page 34).

Mission notes

You will have to play around with the batter ratios; different rice flours give a different crunch. The crispiness also depends on how much water the mushrooms have in them and how much liquid is released from the ginger, garlic and yoghurt. The lower the water content, the crispier the result.

फिश कटलेट

makes 14 croquettes

FISH CUTLETS

Desi spiced fish and potato croquettes with chilli and nigella crust. Crispy on the outside, soft and aromatic on the inside, these croquettes bring the warmth of Indian spices to a classic snack. Perfect as a starter, street food-style treat or party platter. These can be made ahead and stored in the freezer.

INGREDIENTS

For the infused milk

60 ml milk
60 ml cream
1 small bay leaf
1 small garlic clove, smashed
1 whole star anise
½ tsp black peppercorns (6–8 peppercorns)
a pinch of mace
2 green cardamom pods, lightly crushed
½ tsp cumin seeds (1.5 g)
3 g salt

For the fish & potato mix

250 g white fish (cooked weight)
250 g peeled potatoes (cooked weight)
15 g chopped fresh coriander
5 g chopped green chilli
50g red onion, diced small
10 g kadai masala powder
2 g black pepper powder
10g turmeric powder
5 g salt
100 ml infused milk

For the panko crust

100 g panko breadcrumbs
10 g chilli flakes
10 g nigella seeds
15 g chopped fresh coriander
150 g plain flour (for flour slurry)
cold water

For the kadai masala powder

10 g coriander seeds
6 g cumin seeds
6 g dried Kashmiri chillies
6 g fennel seeds
8 g black peppercorns
1 g cinnamon
1 g green cardamom
1 small clove

METHOD

Combine milk and cream in a saucepan with bay leaf, garlic, star anise, peppercorns, mace, cardamom, cumin seeds and salt. Bring to a boil, then simmer for 15–20 minutes. Cool, strain and set aside.

Prepare the fish & potato mix by steaming the fish and boiling the peeled potatoes until both are cooked and tender. Mash together. Gradually stir in the infused milk to bind the mixture, being careful not to make it too wet.

Fold in chopped red onion, coriander, green chilli, kadai masala, black pepper, turmeric powder and salt. Mix thoroughly.

Portion into balls of 35 g. Place on a tray and refrigerate until solid.

Make the kadai masala powder by toasting coriander seeds, cumin seeds, dried chillies, fennel seeds, black peppercorns, cinnamon, cardamom and clove until aromatic. Cool, then grind coarsely and store in an airtight container.

Mix panko breadcrumbs with chilli flakes, nigella seeds and chopped coriander.

For the slurry, whisk flour and cold water into a smooth slurry with the consistency of double cream.

Take chilled balls, coat with seasoned flour, dip into the flour slurry, then roll in the crumb mix. Fry until golden brown and crisp. Serve hot with curry leaf tartare (page 34).

मटन रोल

makes 28

MUTTON ROLLS

Shorteats of Sri Lanka, otherwise known as mutton rolls. Crispy, spiced lamb and potato wrapped in pastry, coated in golden panko and fried until shatteringly crisp. These rolls are crunchy on the outside, soft and masala-packed on the inside, layered with curry leaves, green chillies and a hit of MM garam masala. We first discovered them in Sri Lanka, and while the traditional version uses hand-rolled dough, we've hacked it with spring roll sheets, a shortcut that saves time but still delivers a snack-time legend.

INGREDIENTS

For the filling

100 ml oil
10 g mustard seeds
10 g cumin seeds
400 g red onion, sliced
100 g leeks, chopped
10 g curry leaves
10 g green chillies, chopped
10 g salt
20 g ginger-garlic paste
1 kg coarsely ground mutton mince
10 g pandan leaves
10 g turmeric powder
30 g Madras curry powder
20 g MM garam masala
50 g fresh coriander, chopped
400 g boiled potato, roughly mashed

For the rolls

28 spring roll sheets, frozen (Spring Home brand, large size preferred)
150 g plain flour (for slurry)
cold water, as needed
oil, for deep frying
1 kg Asian-style panko (thick cut, not fine breadcrumbs)
150 g nigella seeds
100 g chilli flakes

METHOD

Heat oil in a wide pan and crackle the mustard and cumin seeds. Add the onions, leeks and curry leaves, then sauté until softened. Stir in the chopped green chillies and salt, cooking until the onions are translucent. Add the ginger-garlic paste and fry until fragrant.

Add the coarse mutton mince and brown it well, stirring to break it up until no raw colour remains. This browning step is crucial for a deep meaty flavour. Add the pandan leaves, turmeric, Madras curry powder and garam masala. Cook until the mince is fully done and the oil separates. Fold in the fresh coriander and mashed potato. Mix well, then set aside to cool completely.

Rolling & coating

For the slurry, whisk flour and cold water into a smooth slurry with the consistency of double cream.

Use about 60 g of cooled filling per spring roll sheet. Roll tightly, folding in the edges. Seal with the slurry.

For the coating, dip each roll into the slurry to coat fully, ensuring the seams are covered.

Mix the panko, nigella seeds and chilli flakes in a tray. Roll each slurry-coated roll in the panko mix, pressing gently so the crumbs stick evenly, especially along the seams.

Chill the coated rolls for at least 30 minutes before frying to help the coating set.

Frying

Heat oil to 170°C. Deep-fry the rolls in batches until golden and crisp. Drain on a wire rack or kitchen paper and serve hot with karma ketchup (page 33)

Mission notes

Freeze any rolls you don't use in an airtight container or ziplock bag. Thaw overnight in the fridge before frying so they crisp up evenly.

कैसे करें
HOW TO: MUTTON ROLL
मटन रोल

How to roll and coat spring rolls

1.
Place the spring roll sheet on your work surface like a diamond, with one corner pointing upwards.

2.
Spoon the filling in a horizontal line across the lower half of the sheet.

3.
Dab a little flour slurry on the bottom corner.

4.
Add small dabs of slurry on the left and right corners.

5.
Fold the right corner over the filling towards the left.

6.
Fold the left corner over towards the right.

7.
Fold the bottom corner upwards over the filling.

8.
Dab slurry on the top corner.

9.
Roll the sheet firmly upwards, pressing gently to secure the filling.

10.
You now have a neat, tightly sealed spring roll ready for coating.

11.
Dip the spring roll fully into the flour slurry.

12.
Place it into the panko breadcrumbs, coating evenly and pressing gently so the crumbs stick all over.

1.
2.
3.
4.
5.
6.
7.
8.
9.
10.
11.
12.

वाटरमैलों चाट
WATERMELON CHAAT

serves 4

A fresh, playful twist on street-style chaat. Sweet, juicy watermelon is pimped up with a spiced fennel and pepper syrup; we add tangy lime and mint-flavoured sour cream finished with roasted cumin, black salt and toasted pumpkin seeds. Sweet, salty, sour and a hint of chilli, all on one plate. Not a classic Indian dish, but an example of our Mission Masala way of adding something fresh to our menus.

INGREDIENTS

For the fennel-pepper spice
50 g fennel seeds
25 g cracked black pepper

For the fennel-pepper syrup
1 tbsp oil
1 tbsp Deggi mirch powder
500 ml water
250 g sugar
100 ml tamarind chutney (see page 28)
1 tbsp fennel-pepper spice (from above)

For the mint sour cream
50 g sour cream
20 g coriander and mint chutney (page 31)
pinch of salt
juice of ½ lime

For the chaat
600 g chopped watermelon
3 tbsp toasted pumpkin seeds
½ tbsp fennel-pepper spice (recipe above)
a handful of fresh mint leaves, for garnish
roasted cumin powder
black salt
zest and juice of ½ lime
10 g fresh mint leaves, finely chopped

METHOD

Dry roast fennel seeds and cracked pepper in a warm pan until fragrant. Pound to a coarse powder using a mortar and pestle. Set aside.

To make the syrup, heat oil in a saucepan and add the Deggi mirch powder. Before it burns, pour in the water. Bring to the boil, then stir in sugar and tamarind chutney. Simmer for 30 minutes until syrupy. Stir in 1 tablespoon of fennel-pepper spice. Refrigerate until completely cooled.

To assemble the chaat, toss the watermelon with a drizzle of the chilled spiced syrup and sprinkle with pumpkin seeds. Dust lightly with black salt and fennel-pepper spice.

Finish with mint sour cream and sprigs of fresh mint.

SILENCE PLEASE
TODDY

DESI
ALL
TURAL
INE
SKY
UM
OKA
COLD LASSI
ROSE LASSI
MIX LASSI

CURRY 'N RICE AND ALL THINGS NICE. THE SOUL OF THE TABLE.

Every home has *that* curry. The one that brings everyone to the table. Growing up, it was what brought us together on Sunday afternoons. Curries are the first thing friends ask us to teach them. They're often rushed, underestimated, or drowned in shortcuts – but when done right, you'll taste the difference.
This chapter is your masterclass in building proper flavour, one layer at a time.
We'll show you the foundations, then hand you the tools to make it your own.
They're messy. They're soulful. They taste like home – even if you didn't grow up eating them.

ASHOKA
Mixed Pickle

START WITH FAT

The fat you choose sets the tone. It's the first flavour carrier and travels all the way through the curry, picking up and passing on everything that follows.

Heat your fat or oil properly before adding anything else – if it's not hot enough, nothing blooms.

SUNFLOWER, VEGETABLE OR GROUNDNUT OIL
Neutral, high smoking points and don't interfere with the flavour of spices

GHEE
Rich, nutty and creamy depth

MUSTARD OIL
Punchy, pungent, bold, sharp, vegan

COCONUT OIL
Light, vegan, sweet and silky

WHOLE SPICES

These go in once your oil is shimmering. Let them crackle and release their aromas.

Don't rush this step. If the spices burn, the whole dish will taste off. If they don't pop or sizzle, the oil isn't hot enough yet.

BLACK MUSTARD SEEDS
Pungent, earthy, nutty

CURRY LEAVES
Fragrant, herbaceous, aromatic

CUMIN SEEDS
Earthy, warm, nutty

BAY LEAF
Woody, herbal, subtle

GREEN CARDAMOM
Herbal, aromatic, spiced

BLACK CARDAMOM
Smoky, intense, robust

CLOVES
Warm, peppery and numbing lingering warmth

CINNAMON
Sweet, woody, fragrant

FENNEL SEEDS
Sweet, liquoricey, cooling

STAR ANISE
Bold, liquoricey, aromatic

AJWAIN (CAROM SEEDS)
Herby, warmth and savoury

THE ONIONS

This is the foundation of most curries, except in dishes like butter chicken or paneer makhani, where onions are left out entirely.

SHALLOTS
Mild, sweet, delicate
For light or coconut-based curries

RED ONIONS
Sharp, vibrant, slightly sweet
For punchy southern dishes with colour and bite

YELLOW ONIONS
Savoury, robust, caramel-friendly
For north Indian gravies, deep browing and building depth

LEEKS
Sweet, mellow, oniony
For creamy and buttery veg, lentil stews and gentle depth

SPRING ONIONS
Fresh, grassy, mild
For stir-fried curries and lighter dishes

Cut & texture:

Slice, dice or chop – but remember:
How you cut and cook your onions shapes the curry's body, depth and texture.

How to cook them right:

Deep golden: Low and slow, with lid on → jammy onions. This draws out sweetness and creates a soft, melt-in texture.
Want crispy onions? Cook on high heat, uncovered. Great for garnishes or when you want a bit of crunch layered into the dish (e.g. biryani toppings, final tadka).

Don't rush this step. Underdone onions taste raw and throw off the balance of the dish.

Overdone or burnt ones make it bitter.

Get this right and you're already 50% there.

Salt your onions while cooking to draw out moisture and help caramelise them faster. Too dry too fast? Add a splash of water if they're catching or browning before softening. Onion water content varies, so some need help staying moist while they cook.

GINGER, GARLIC AND GREEN CHILLI

These go in only after your onions are fully cooked. Adding them too early leads to raw, harsh flavours and means they'll steam instead of fry, especially if your onions are still releasing water.

At this stage, add your green chilli too: finely chopped, sliced, slit lengthwise or whole.

This allows the chilli to gently fry alongside the ginger and garlic, infusing the oil with heat and aroma.

Adjust the amount and type of chilli to your heat preference.

Don't remove the seeds if you want milder spice – just add less.

Cut:

Paste: Smooth, quick to cook and ideal for blended sauces.
Finely chopped or grated: Melts into the base but still gives a bit of texture.
Julienned: For bite and texture in the curry itself, or add at the end for a fresh zing in richer dishes like lamb curry.

POWDERED SPICES

This is where your depth comes from:

TURMERIC
Earthy, bitter, grounding. For depth and colour

CORIANDER POWDER
Citrusy, nutty, mellow. For building gentle body

CUMIN POWDER
Warm, earthy, smoky. Brings depth and savoury notes

ROASTED CUMIN POWDER
Toasty, nutty, bold. Adds punchy aroma

CHILLI POWDER
Hot, sharp, warming. For heat and colour; adjust to taste and region

BLACK OR WHITE PEPPER
Pungent, spicy, sharp. Black is bolder and aromatic, white is milder and muskier

Toast them briefly and you'll smell them release their aroma.

They should almost start to catch at the bottom of the pan – that's your cue to stop.

Don't let them burn. The next ingredient (usually tomato or water) will deglaze the pan.

करी मास्टरक्लास
CURRY MASTERCLASS

HOW TO COOK A CURRY: THE BLUEPRINT

Please take your time to read and understand this before skipping to the recipes

This is your masterclass, framework and tool for experimenting to make your very own curry. If you want a curry in which you can taste the depth and combination of ingredients, you need to layer your flavours one step at a time. The method is simple, but it can't be rushed. This is your go-to guide.

TOMATO

This step cools the pan and gives body to your base. Tomatoes = tang + depth.

Cook them down until the oil comes to the surface and splits off the base – this is how you know it's done.

Don't rush this: raw tomato ruins a curry.

CANNED TOMATOES
Tangy and deep, for consistent flavour

FRESH CHOPPED TOMATOES
Juicy, bright, chunks add body

FRESH BLITZED TOMATOES
Light and fresh for a soft tomato presence

TOMATO PURÉE
Concentrated and intense, used in small amounts for colour and umami depth

TAMARIND WATER
Tangy, fruity and earthy sourness

ADD YOUR MAIN

This is when your star ingredient goes in: it can be raw, pre-cooked or marinated, depending on the dish.

Your base masala is ready by now: it's time to introduce the main and build the final layer of flavour.

What qualifies as "main" here:

MARINATED CHICKEN
Raw or grilled

PANEER
Grilled or pan-fried

VEGETABLES
Chopped or pre-roasted

TOFU, MUSHROOMS OR SOYA

PRAWNS, FISH OR SQUID

EGGS
Boiled, peeled, optionally shallow-fried in spiced oil

LAMB, GOAT OR BEEF
Raw or slow-cooked

Key technique:

Once added, your main needs to coat well in the masala.

This isn't just tossing, but about letting the base cling, roast slightly and deepen the flavour before any liquid comes in.

Let it sit in the pan, on medium heat and soak in the spices – don't rush this.

This step seals the flavour and allows everything to come together.

BINDER OR LIQUID

Now it's time to bring it together: this step is part of the finishing stage. Your main is cooked through and coated in the masala, flavours are emulsified into a cohesive sauce and now it's time to bind it into the final curry.

Choose your liquid based on the dish:

WATER
Used when the masala is already rich and you want a runny curry to serve with rice rather than bread

COCONUT MILK OR CREAM
Adds a mellow and rounded sweetness

YOGHURT
(whisked)
Choose full-fat yoghurt only for less tang. Use gentle heat and stir it in gradually.

NUT PASTES
(cashew, almond)
Add thickness, richness and a subtle sweetness

Technique:

Simmer gently, not rapidly, as this helps the curry stay glossy and tender.

Add water only as needed, bit by bit, to loosen the curry to your preferred consistency.

This is the stage where your curry becomes complete, not just in texture, but in balance. It should taste rounded, well-integrated and ready to finish.

FINISH AND LAYER FRESHNESS

Right at the end of cooking, add:

GARAM MASALA
For warm and aromatic notes. Used sparingly as it can become bitter if cooked too long

DRIED FENUGREEK LEAVES
(dried methi)
Wonderful earthy aroma. Add it at the end to preserve its delicate flavour and avoid bitterness

LEMON JUICE OR VINEGAR
(optional)
For brightening Indian curries. Use vinegar sparingly and only if it suits the recipe

CORIANDER LEAVES
FRESH CURRY LEAVES
Green herbs for vibrant freshness and colour

Always taste and tweak at this stage – balance is everything.

ओल्ड स्कूल चिकन करी

OLD SCHOOL CHICKEN CURRY

serves 6

This is a proper homestyle chicken curry, with a full-flavoured masala built on slow-fried onions and real spice. Every house from every region has its own version. Spices and ratios may vary from home to home, but the main formula remains very similar. This is the kind of curry that gets better as it rests: leftovers hit harder the next day. You can swap the coconut milk for yoghurt if you prefer a more tangy, northern-style finish. Marinate any meat or protein in this gravy; it will go great with any alternative that you pick.

INGREDIENTS

For the chicken marinade

1.2 kg chicken thighs, chopped into 4–5 cm chunks
100 g ginger-garlic paste
2 tsp turmeric
1½ tsp salt
juice of ½ lime

For the curry base

50 g vegetable oil
2 tbsp cumin seeds
8–10 green cardamom pods
5 bay leaves
2 small sticks cinnamon (about 3 cm each)
600 g red onion, finely chopped
2 tsp Himalayan pink salt
60 g ginger-garlic paste
600 g tomatoes, pulverised or blended smooth
2 tsp turmeric
1½ tbsp Deggi mirch (red Kashmiri chilli powder)
3 tbsp coriander powder

To finish

1 tsp garam masala
2 tsp green chillies, finely chopped (adjust according to taste)
2 tbsp fresh coriander, chopped
200 ml coconut milk

METHOD

Marinate the chicken thighs with ginger-garlic paste, turmeric, salt and lime juice. Let sit for at least 30 minutes or longer while you prep the base.

Heat oil in a heavy-bottomed pot. Add cumin seeds, cardamom pods, bay leaves and cinnamon. Let the spices bloom in the oil until fragrant.

Add the onions and salt. Cook on medium heat until the water has left the onions and they become a deep golden brown. Take your time, as this is your flavour foundation.

Add the ginger-garlic paste and fry for a minute until the raw smell disappears. Pour in the tomatoes and cook down until the oil starts to separate; this can take 10–15 minutes. Stir often.

Add turmeric, Deggi mirch and coriander powder. Fry the spices for a minute or two until aromatic.

Now add the marinated chicken. Sear it in the masala, turning to coat every piece well. Let it cook, uncovered, for a few minutes to lock in the flavour.

Add water to cover and simmer gently until the chicken is tender and the curry has thickened, about 20–25 minutes. Add garam masala and stir, let it get absorbed into the gravy for a few minutes. Stir in the green chillies and coconut milk. Simmer for another 2–3 minutes.

Finish with fresh coriander. Taste and adjust seasoning. It should be spicy, earthy and full of soul.

तमिल कोस्टल प्रॉन करी

TAMIL PRAWN CURRY

serves 6

Tangy tamarind, tomato, green chilli, coriander and turmeric. A bold, tangy, South Indian coastal gravy, layered with spice – this curry delivers coastal flavour with grilled prawns and a rich, tamarind-forward base. Finished with sizzling tadka for that final lift.

INGREDIENTS

For the prawns

75 g oil
30 g Deggi mirch powder
22 g coriander powder
15 g turmeric powder
45 g ginger-garlic paste
30 g lemon juice
7½ g salt
1 kg prawns

For the curry base

225 ml oil
½ tsp cumin seeds
½ tsp fennel seeds
½ tsp fenugreek seeds
1½ tsp chopped green chilli
600 g red onion, chopped
525 g tinned tomato, blended (a good-quality tin, or use fresh if it's tomato season)
1½ tbsp Deggi mirch powder
1½ tbsp coriander powder
¾ tsp turmeric powder
¾ tsp cumin powder
1½ tbsp ginger-garlic paste
tamarind water (60 g tamarind soaked in 300 ml hot water, strained)
1 tbsp salt (plus to taste)
150 ml fish stock
water to adjust consistency

For the tadka (tempering)

2 tbsp oil
½ tsp mustard seeds
½ tsp cumin seeds
1 tsp curry leaves
½ tsp dry red chillies

To serve

15 g chopped coriander leaves

METHOD

Marinate the prawns

Mix the prawns with the oil, spices, lemon juice and salt. Let it sit for at least 1 hour, longer if possible.

Build the curry base

In a heavy-bottomed pot, heat the oil. Add cumin seeds, fennel seeds and fenugreek and let them crackle. Stir in the green chilli and onion and cook until onions have released most of their water and are browned. Add the ginger-garlic paste and cook until the raw smell goes. Add the tomato and cook well, then stir in all the powdered masala and keep cooking until the oil begins to separate. Pour in the tamarind water and cook for 10 minutes until it comes together into a thick masala paste. Transfer the mixture to a blender and blend into a smooth paste.

Add your spices: Deggi mirch, coriander powder, turmeric and cumin powder. Cook until the masala is rich and aromatic.

Pour in the tamarind water and simmer for around 10 minutes to concentrate the flavour. Blend the mixture with a hand blender until smooth, or transfer to a countertop blender, blitz until smooth and then return it to the pot.

Add fish stock and enough water to get your curry to the right consistency. Simmer again and season with salt to taste.

Grill the prawns

Grill or sear the marinated prawns over high heat in a grill pan, over an open fire or on a hot skillet. Grill until they're just cooked and slightly charred (see BBQ section). Or drop them as they are, raw, into the cooked gravy and cook for 2–3 minutes.

Finish with tadka

Heat oil in a small pan. Add mustard seeds, cumin seeds, curry leaves and dry red chillies. Let them crackle and bloom, then pour the hot tadka over the curry and stir.

Serve it up

Spoon the hot curry into a bowl or platter. Top with grilled prawns and fresh coriander. Serve with steamed rice or buttery parathas.

Mission notes

Tamarind brings that deep, sour-savoury hit – don't skip it. The curry base can be made a day ahead. Reheat gently and add the grilled prawns to serve.

Try with different fish or mixed seafood.

Just before serving, finish with a squeeze of lemon or a dash of vinegar if you want to add some bite.

कर्मा कोरमा चिकन

KARMA KORMA CHICKEN

serves 6

Creamy, rich and gently spiced, this korma is aromatic and full of flavour, with brown onion paste, a cashew-poppy base and a touch of coconut. Regal, comforting, deeply satisfying and finished with a gentle perfume of rose water. The soaked cashew and poppy seed paste give this korma its signature silky texture. You can replace chicken with paneer, vegetables or koftas; the base works beautifully with all.

INGREDIENTS

For the chicken and marinade

1.2 kg boneless chicken thighs, cut into large chunks
30 g neutral oil
1 tbsp ginger-garlic paste
100 g yoghurt
1 tsp turmeric
½ tsp salt

For the onion paste

100 ml oil
200 g white onion, sliced
100 ml water

For the quick nut and spice paste

120 g cashews
20 g poppy seeds
80 ml water

For the base

3 tbsp oil
2 bay leaves
3 green cardamom pods
4 black peppercorns
3 cloves
2 blades mace
1 cinnamon stick
35 g ginger-garlic paste
200 g yoghurt, whisked
¾ tbsp Deggi mirch
1½ tbsp coriander powder
¾ tbsp turmeric powder
salt to taste
400 ml coconut milk
100 ml coconut cream

To finish

2 tsp ground cardamom mace mix (70% cardamom, 30% mace)
40 g butter
40 ml fresh cream
1 tsp rose water

METHOD

Marinate the chicken with oil, ginger-garlic paste, yoghurt, turmeric and salt. Set aside for at least 30 minutes while you prep the base.

Fry the onions until they're golden brown and crispy. Blend them with 100 ml water into a smooth paste, then set aside.

Blend the cashews and poppy seeds with the water into a smooth paste; set aside.

Heat the oil in a heavy-bottomed pot. Add bay leaves, cardamom, peppercorns, cloves, mace and cinnamon. Fry until aromatic. Add the ginger-garlic paste and sauté briefly.

Add the cashew paste to the pan together with the whisked yoghurt, Deggi mirch, coriander, turmeric and salt. Cook gently for 15 minutes until you have a smooth paste with all the spices emulsified.

Stir the onion paste into the pot and cook for 3–5 minutes.

Pour in coconut milk and coconut cream. Simmer on low heat for 5–10 minutes.

Add the marinated chicken. Simmer on medium-low heat for 20–25 minutes until the chicken is tender and the sauce has thickened.

Stir in the cardamom and mace mix. Cook for 2–3 minutes. Remove from heat. Swirl in butter, fresh cream and rose water.

पीनट चिकन करी

PEANUT CHICKEN CURRY

serves 4

An Indo-Malay dish that travelled West with the Mamaks (Muslims) of India and fuses South and East Asian flavours. Creamy, spicy, nutty and bold, this satay chicken comes with a rich sauce made from roasted peanuts, chillies, coconut milk and dark soy. Serve it with jasmine rice, herbs, extra chilli and cold beer. It's street food comfort, done proper.

INGREDIENTS

For the satay seasoning

1½ tsp coriander
1½ tsp cumin powder
1½ tsp turmeric
1½ tsp paprika (sweet or normal, not smoked or spicy)
1¼ tsp chilli powder
3½ tsp madras curry powder (not hot)
1¼ tsp salt (cooking/kosher) or 1 tsp table salt
2 tsp white sugar

For the chicken

1 tbsp oil
750 g chicken thigh fillets, cut into bite-size pieces
½ onion (brown, white or yellow), grated

For the satay sauce

1 tbsp oil (for sauce)
3–6 bird's eye chillies or other small red chillies, finely chopped
¼ cup onion (brown, white or yellow), finely diced
4 garlic cloves, minced
remaining satay seasoning
1 cup chicken stock
¾ cup roasted unsalted peanuts, chopped and divided
2 tsp kecap manis
3 tsp dark soy sauce
400 g coconut milk (full-fat preferred)
2 tbsp peanut butter (pure or spreadable, crunchy or smooth)
1 lemongrass stalk (white part only, smashed) or 3 kaffir lime leaves
about 2 tbsp lime juice, to taste

To serve (optional)

chopped peanuts
coriander leaves
fresh red chilli, finely chopped
steamed jasmine or plain rice

METHOD

Satay seasoning

Mix all the satay seasoning ingredients together in a small bowl.

Add 3½ tablespoons of the seasoning to the chicken along with the grated onion. Mix well and marinate for at least 3 hours, preferably overnight.

Chicken

Heat the oil in a non-stick pan over high heat. Cook the chicken in two batches until browned all over but still slightly raw inside. Transfer to a bowl, cover and keep warm.

Satay sauce

Using the same pan, turn the heat down to medium and add 1 tbsp oil. Add the chilli, onion and garlic. Sauté for about 2 minutes until the onion is translucent. Add the remaining satay seasoning and cook for 1 minute. Transfer the mixture to a small blender or food processor. Add the chicken stock and half the chopped peanuts. Blend until mostly smooth – a few peanut chunks are fine.

Return the sauce mixture to the pan. Add the remaining ¼ cup peanuts, kecap manis, dark soy sauce, coconut milk and peanut butter. Stir to combine.

Add your flavour infusion: either bruised lemongrass or torn kaffir lime leaves. Return the browned chicken to the sauce. Bring to a simmer. Lower the heat and simmer gently for 15 minutes until the sauce thickens and the chicken is fully cooked.

Add lime juice to taste. Serve hot with jasmine or plain rice. Garnish with extra peanuts, fresh coriander and more chilli if you like.

Mission notes

This dish keeps well and gets better the next day.

For extra depth, toast the peanuts before using.

You can swap chicken for beef, tofu, prawns or mushrooms – just be sure to adjust cooking times accordingly.

Great with pickled cucumber or a shredded green mango salad on the side.

dian
ADING CO.

कीमा स्लॉपी जो

KEEMA SLOPPY JOE

serves 6

This is not your school canteen sloppy joe. This sloppy joe starts with a spiced lamb keema, stuffed into a toasted buttery bun, finished with melted mozzarella, tangy tamarind sauce and in true Mission Masala style we added some extras like a punchy chimichurri tempered with curry leaves and mustard seeds and chopped pickled jalapeños. It's the kind of sandwich you need both hands (and a napkin) for. It's soft, saucy and totally addictive.

INGREDIENTS

For the keema filling

3 tbsp oil
600g lamb mince
1 cinnamon stick
2 green cardamom pods
2 cloves
1 bay leaf
2 onions (approx. 250g), finely chopped
1 tbsp ginger-garlic paste
2 green chillies, chopped
1 tsp cumin powder
1 tsp coriander powder
1 tsp turmeric powder
1 tsp Deggi mirch or paprika
2 tomatoes (approx. 300g), blended
salt, to taste
small bunch fresh coriander, chopped

For the Indian chimichurri

30g fresh coriander
20g fresh mint
2 green chillies
2 tbsp vinegar
2 tbsp oil
salt, to taste
1 tbsp oil
1 tsp mustard seeds
10 curry leaves

To assemble

6 brioche buns or pav buns
6 mozzarella slices
tamarind sauce (see page 28)
4 tbsp pickled jalapeños, chopped
extra coriander leaves
60 g of anything like bombay mix (see page 17)

METHOD

Heat 1 tbsp oil in a wide pan. Add the lamb mince and cook over medium-high heat until browned all over, breaking it up with a spoon. Remove from the pan and set aside.

In the same pan, add the remaining oil. Drop in the cinnamon stick, cardamom, cloves and bay leaf, letting them crackle. Stir in the onions and fry until golden brown. Add the ginger-garlic paste and green chillies, cooking off the raw edge.

Sprinkle in the cumin, coriander, turmeric and Deggi mirch. Fry briefly until fragrant. Stir in the blended tomatoes, season with salt and cook until the oil splits.

Return the browned mince to the pan, mixing it into the masala. Simmer until tender and coated. Stir through chopped coriander and adjust seasoning.

For the chimichurri, blitz coriander, mint, chillies, vinegar, oil and salt into a coarse paste. Heat 1 tbsp oil in a small pan, add mustard seeds and curry leaves until they pop, then stir this tempering into the chutney.

To assemble, lightly toast the buns. Pile hot keema onto the base, top with a mozzarella slice and place under a hot grill to let it melt. Remove when cheese has melted, drizzle with tamarind sauce, spoon over chimichurri, scatter with chopped pickled jalapeños and finish with fresh coriander. Garnish with your bombay mix and close the bun. Serve immediately.

ब्लैक पेपर बीफ़ टाकोस

serves 6

KERALA PEPPER BEEF TACOS

We love any excuse to turn a curry into a taco and this Kerala-style beef works perfectly. The slow-cooked beef is tender, the masala is rich with roasted spices, coconut oil and curry leaves and the coarsely ground black pepper gives it a fiery kick. Served on a warm paratha with fresh toppings, it's everything you love about a hearty South Indian curry in taco form.

INGREDIENTS

For the braised beef in aromatic stock

1.2 kg beef cubes (cut into 20 g pieces)
1 cinnamon stick
1 green cardamom
1 bay leaf
2 cloves
1 tsp coriander powder (5 g)
½ tsp turmeric powder (3 g)
½ tsp cumin powder (3 g)
½ tsp garam masala (2 g)
1 tsp ginger-garlic paste (5 g)
1 tsp salt (5 g)
water, to cover

For the pepper masala

125 g whole black pepper
50 g whole coriander seeds
50 g whole cumin seeds

For the curry masala base

30 ml vegetable oil
30 ml coconut oil
300 g red onions, sliced
10 g ginger-garlic paste
125 g tinned tomatoes, blended
1 tsp green chilli, chopped
3 pcs star anise
1 cinnamon stick (5 cm)
2 green cardamom pods
2 g cloves
3 g fresh curry leaves
3–4 dry whole red chillies
1 tsp Deggi mirch
1 tsp garam masala
½ tsp turmeric powder
1 tsp coriander powder
15 g pepper masala (recipe above)
25 g fresh coriander, chopped
salt, to taste

For the taco elements

150 g white cabbage, shredded
75 g carrot, julienned
50 g red onion, thinly sliced
2 tbsp fresh mint, chopped
1 tsp chaat masala
½ tsp Deggi
juice of ½ lime
200 ml South Indian pickling liquid (see page 37)
15 paratha bases from page 43 (make smaller ones for the tacos, or use small flour tortillas)
mint mayo (see page 31)
pickled yellow silver onions (see page 37)
fresh coriander leaves, for garnish
extra lime wedges, for serving

METHOD

Braise the beef in a pot. Combine beef cubes with the spices, salt and ginger-garlic paste. Cover with water and bring to a gentle simmer. Cook for about 45 minutes, until the beef is tender. Reserve the cooking stock.

Prepare the pepper masala by roasting the pepper, coriander and cumin seeds. Grind coarsely; it should be textured, not a fine powder.

To make the curry masala base, start by heating vegetable oil and coconut oil together in a heavy-bottomed pan. Add star anise, cinnamon, cardamom, cloves, curry leaves and dry red chillies. Fry until aromatic and all the spices are infused in the oil.

Add sliced onions and sauté until deep golden brown. Be patient with the onions; give them as long as they need to brown. Stir in ginger-garlic paste and fry briefly. Add the blended tomato and keep cooking until the oil separates.

Spice it up by adding Deggi mirch, turmeric, coriander powder and garam masala. Fry until the raw aroma disappears, then switch off the heat.

Remove 60% of the cooked masala base, blend into a smooth paste, then return it to the pan. Mix with the unblended masala for texture. Keeping some of it unblended will ensure that it doesn't become a runny curry with gravy. Stir in chopped coriander. Taste and adjust salt (remember that the beef and stock are already seasoned).

Add the braised beef and a splash of reserved stock to loosen slightly (keep it thick so it will stay in the tacos). Stir in 15 g of pepper masala. Simmer 2–3 minutes, then switch off. Shred the beef lightly with two forks.

For the final pepper hit, stir in the coarsely ground pepper masala. Mix gently, then remove from the heat.

To make the coleslaw, toss cabbage, carrot, red onion, mint, chaat masala, Deggi mirch, lime juice and South Indian pickling liquid. Let sit 10 minutes to allow the flavours to combine.

Warm paratha bases or tortillas. On each base, spread a spoonful of mint mayo, add about 40 g shredded pepper beef, then top with coleslaw, pickled yellow silver onions and fresh coriander leaves. Serve with lime wedges.

मोइली मसल्स

MOILEE MUSSELS

serves 4 as starter
2 as main course

A coastal coconut curry with fresh mussels, turmeric and green chilli. Light, fragrant and full of flavour – this one's fast but fancy.

INGREDIENTS

2 tbsp coconut oil
1 tsp mustard seeds
10 curry leaves
1 small onion, sliced
10 g ginger, julienned
2 green chillies, slit
5 g turmeric
200 ml coconut milk
100 ml water
1 kg fresh mussels, cleaned and beards removed
juice of half a lime
salt to taste
fresh coriander to garnish

METHOD

Heat coconut oil in a deep pan. Add mustard seeds and let them pop. Add curry leaves, onion, ginger and green chillies. Cook gently until softened. Add turmeric and stir for 30 seconds. Pour in coconut milk and water. Bring to a gentle simmer.

Add mussels, cover and cook for 3–4 minutes until they open. Discard any unopened mussels. Squeeze in lime and adjust salt.

Garnish with coriander and serve immediately.

Mission notes

Fast, fragrant and perfect for crusty bread or appams.
Don't overcook the mussels – once they open, they're done.

Storage

In the fridge for up to a day (shells removed).
Best eaten fresh.
Don't store the mussels in the freezer.

ओबेर्गिणे एंड पोटैटो करी

ALOO BHENGAN SABJI

serves 4

Chunky, soft aubergine tossed through a spiced onion masala with buttery potatoes, coriander stalks and a choice of yoghurt or butter at the end. Homely, humble and the perfect kind of sabji to scoop up with warm roti or try stuffed into a toastie with a store-bought mango or chilli pickle and sharp cheddar. Goes great with paratha, plain rice, or alongside a simple dhal.

INGREDIENTS

400 g aubergine
1 tbsp ghee
1 tbsp cumin seeds
400 g red onion, finely diced
a small handful of coriander stalks, finely chopped
1 tbsp ginger-garlic paste
150 g potato, peeled and diced small
1 tsp turmeric powder
2 tsp coriander powder
1 tsp cumin powder
1 fresh tomato, chopped
salt, to taste
a splash of water, if needed

To finish

1 tbsp yoghurt or butter

METHOD

Chop the aubergine into 3–4 cm chunks. Cover the bottom of a pan in oil, put on medium heat and fry the aubergine until golden. Set aside.

In another pan, heat the ghee and add the cumin seeds. Let them sizzle and infuse the fat.

Add the onions and coriander stalks with a pinch of salt. Cook on medium heat until softened and beginning to colour. Stir in the ginger-garlic paste and fry for a minute until fragrant.

Add the potatoes along with turmeric, coriander powder and cumin powder. Stir to coat the potatoes in the masala. If the spices begin to catch on the bottom, loosen with a splash of water. Cook until the potatoes are almost cooked through; they should break but not crumble when pressed with a spoon.

Add the chopped tomato and cook until broken down and jammy; the oil should just be starting to release again.

Now add in the fried aubergine. Stir gently so they don't break too much. Cover and cook on low heat for 10–15 minutes until the potatoes are tender and the sabji is fully melted.

Taste and adjust salt.

Finish with either a dollop of yoghurt or a spoonful of butter stirred in right before serving, depending on your mood.

मलाई कोफ्ता

makes 14 koftas

MALAI KOFTA

Rich, nutty paneer dumplings stuffed with nuts and raisins, fried golden in a velvety cashew gravy. This one is an indulgent and regal vegetarian show stopper.

INGREDIENTS

For the paneer kofta (~35 g each)
- 300 g paneer, finely grated
- 50 g raisins, chopped
- 50 g cashew nuts, chopped
- 2 tsp green chilli, finely chopped (10 g)
- 2 tsp fresh coriander, chopped (10 g)
- 1 tsp Deggi mirch powder (5 g)
- 1 tsp coriander powder (5 g)
- ½ tsp garam masala (2 g)
- 2 tbsp plain flour (20 g approximately, for binding)
- 1 tsp salt
- oil, for frying

For the kofta gravy
- 100 ml oil
- 50 g garlic, chopped
- 50 g ginger, chopped
- 500 g OT masala (see recipe below)
- 80 g roasted cashew nut paste
- 2 tsp kasoori methi, crushed (6 g)
- 50–60 ml fresh cream (adjust for consistency)
- 2 tsp fresh coriander, chopped (10 g)
- salt, to taste

For the onion tomato masala (aka OT masala)
- 40 ml oil
- 4 g cumin seeds
- ½ cinnamon stick (about 2 cm)
- 1 small bay leaf
- 2 g cardamom pods (2–3 pods)
- 1 clove (about ¼ g)
- 400 g sliced onions
- 1 tsp salt
- 50 g ginger-garlic paste
- 500 g whole good-quality tinned tomatoes
- ½ tsp turmeric (5 g)
- 1 tsp Deggi mirch (7 g)
- 1 tbsp coriander powder (10 g)

METHOD

Kofta

Mix grated paneer with raisins, cashew nuts, green chilli, coriander and spices, and add flour gradually until the mixture binds. Roll into 14 balls of about 35 g each (golf-ball size). Compress in your palms so that the balls set.

Fry the koftas in medium-hot oil until golden and crisp with the centres cooked through. Drain on paper.

OT Masala

Heat the oil in a heavy pan. Add cumin, cinnamon, bay leaf, cardamom and clove and fry until they crackle. Add sliced onions with salt and cook until light golden.

Stir in the ginger-garlic paste, then add turmeric, Deggi mirch and coriander powder. Add 50 ml water to prevent sticking and cook until aromatic. Add blended tomatoes and cook on medium flame for 35–40 minutes until thick and oil separates. Adjust seasoning.

Use 500 g of this masala for the kofta gravy. Extra keeps well frozen.

Gravy

Heat oil in a pan and fry the chopped garlic and ginger until fragrant. Stir in the OT masala and simmer for 5–6 minutes.

Add cashew nut paste, stir for 1–2 minutes and then add the fresh cream. Simmer gently to a smooth, creamy consistency. Finish with kasoori methi and fresh coriander. Season to taste.

The koftas are best fried and added to the gravy at the last moment so they stay light and don't break apart. Slip them into the warm gravy and coat gently.

Mission notes

OT masala is the true backbone of the restaurant. Make a larger batch, freeze in 500 g packs and pull out as needed for curries!

ओकरा सब्जी

serves 4

OKRA (PINDI) SABJI

This is a stir-fry sabji that celebrates okra at its best. Lightly spiced, gently cooked with soft onions and golden garlic, this one keeps the okra fresh and tender without it turning slimy. Finished with a squeeze of lemon, it's bright and simple and goes really well with a light dhal.

INGREDIENTS

3 tbsp oil
1 tsp cumin seeds
3–4 garlic cloves, sliced
400 g white onion, thinly sliced
½ tomato, finely chopped
1–2 green chillies chopped finely
1 tsp chilli powder, to taste
1 tsp turmeric powder
1 tsp coriander powder
1 tsp cumin powder
1 tsp salt, to taste
400 g okra, trimmed and cut diagonally into 2–3 cm pieces
½ lemon, juiced

METHOD

Heat oil on medium to high heat in a wide pan or a wok. Add the cumin seeds until they sizzle. Stir in the garlic and fry gently until golden. Add the onions and cook until soft and lightly golden at the edges.

Add the powdered spices and salt and stir well. Mix in the tomato and green chilli and cook until it breaks down. Fold in the okra and coat everything in the masala. Cook on medium heat, stirring occasionally, until the okra is tender and the onions fully softened. Keep the lid off throughout, as covering will make the okra slimy. If the pan feels too dry, add a splash more oil rather than water. Finish with a squeeze of lemon juice to brighten the flavour and stop it from sticking.

राजमा केसादिल्ला

RAAJMA QUESADILLA

makes 6

This red kidney bean curry is all about slow-simmered spice, creamy texture, and a masala that clings to every bite. Indian-style refried beans are the ultimate comfort food when slapped into a paratha with melted cheese, sour cream and the perfect chilli mayo.

INGREDIENTS

For the taajma dhal filling

30 ml sunflower oil
1 tsp cumin seeds
2 green cardamom pods
1 bay leaf
1 small cinnamon stick (about 1½ cm)
1 star anise
1 clove
135 g diced red onion
1 tbsp ginger-garlic paste
12 g green chilli, chopped
110 g tomato, chopped
1 tbsp coriander powder
2 tsp cumin powder
1 tsp turmeric powder
1 tsp MM garam masala
1 tbsp chana masala powder
30 g salt (adjust to taste)
400 g tinned red kidney beans (drained weight)

For the build

cooked raajma dhal
480 g mozzarella & cheddar mix, grated
120 g sour cream
20 g mixed pickle (blitzed smooth, then stirred into sour cream)
90 g diced red onion
90 g pickled red onion (see page 37)
6 lime wedges
30 g fresh coriander, chopped (half for filling and half for garnish)
6 parathas (see recipe, page 43) or store-bought flatbreads
butter or ghee, for toasting

METHOD

Cooking the raajma

Heat the sunflower oil in a pan over medium heat. Add the cumin seeds, cardamom pods, bay leaf, cinnamon, star anise and clove. Let them sizzle and infuse the oil for about 30 seconds.

Toss in the red onions with a pinch of salt. Fry until golden brown and softened – don't rush this step. Add the ginger-garlic paste and chopped green chilli. Fry for another minute until the raw smell disappears. Add the tomatoes.

Cook them down until the oil starts to separate and the tomatoes have darkened for about 10–12 minutes. Sprinkle in all the ground spices: coriander, cumin, turmeric, chana masala and garam masala. Stir and toast the spices for a minute until fragrant.

Add the red kidney beans along with a splash of water or bean liquor (if using tinned). Simmer gently on low heat for 15–20 minutes to allow the beans to soak up the masala.

Mash a few beans to naturally thicken the curry. Taste and adjust salt and spice levels to finish.

Building the quesadilla

Mix the sour cream with the blitzed pickle to make a tangy sour cream sauce. Keep the raajma, cheese, diced onion, coriander and lime ready in bowls for easy assembly.

Place a flat, heavy pan or tawa over medium heat. Add a touch of butter or ghee.

Lay one paratha in the pan. Spread roughly 65 g of raajma evenly over half the base. Sprinkle 80 g of cheese mix on top. Add a spoonful of diced red onion and a sprinkle of chopped coriander.

Fold the paratha over into a half-moon. Press lightly with a spatula to seal. Toast until golden and crisp, then flip and repeat on the other side until the cheese is melted.

Remove from the pan, cut in half, top with chilli sour cream, pickled onions and coriander, and serve hot with a squeeze of lime. Repeat for all 6 quesadillas.

कोकोनट दाल
CURRIED COCONUT DHAL

serves 6

A proper dhal with a curry-style base – soft lentils, fried spices, rich and creamy. With a garlicky temper poured over just before serving, it shines. This one's simple, soulful and full of flavour. Easy midweek dinner or batch-cooked and frozen.

INGREDIENTS

250 g red lentils (washed until water runs clear)
1 red onion, finely chopped
1 large tomato, chopped
1 tsp turmeric
1 tsp salt
1 green chilli, whole (or 2 dried red chillies)
1.2 l water (more if needed at the end to adjust thickness)
1 tsp coriander powder
½ tsp garam masala
½ tsp red chilli powder
salt to taste
2 tbsp oil, ghee or coconut oil
1 tsp mustard seeds
½ tsp asafoetida powder
1 tsp cumin seeds
2 garlic cloves, sliced
1 thumb-sized piece of ginger, grated
fresh coriander, chopped
lime to finish

METHOD

Wash the lentils well. Add to a pot with onions, tomatoes, turmeric, salt, green chilli and water. Bring to a boil and simmer until soft and broken down. Skim off any foam as needed. Simmer for 20 minutes on a low moderate heat. Half-cover the pot with the lid – take care that it doesn't boil over.

Add the coriander powder, garam masala, red chilli powder and a pinch more salt into the lentils.

Let it simmer for another 5–10 minutes to bring the flavours together.

In a separate pan, heat oil and add mustard seeds, asafoetida powder and cumin seeds. Let them sputter.

Add sliced garlic and grated ginger. Sauté for 2–3 minutes until fragrant. Pour this temper over the dhal and add the coconut milk and bring to a boil. Garnish with fresh coriander and a squeeze of lime.

Mission notes

The green chilli goes in whole so you get warmth without overpowering the dhal – remove before serving or mash it in for extra fire.

For a thinner, plainer dhal, you can skip the coconut milk – but do use it if you want that lush, velvety finish.

Add toasted seeds for extra crunch or a dollop of thick yoghurt for a fresh note.

Freezes well and gets better the next day.

मिशन पुलाव

serves 4

MISSION PILAU

Aromatic rice cooked low and slow with whole spices, saffron and a buttery onion base. Light but never bland – this is the kind of rice that soaks up sauce and holds its own.

INGREDIENTS

40 g vegetable ghee
25 g ginger-garlic paste
2 garlic cloves
2 green cardamom pods
1 small star anise
1 short cinnamon stick
1 bay leaf
½ blade mace
2 tsp pilau spice mix
290 g basmati rice, rinsed until water runs clear, soaked 20 minutes
400 ml water
15 g salt
pinch of saffron threads or ¼ saffron pellet, soaked in 1 tbsp warm water
1 tbsp rose water
15 g sliced & fried onions (crispy, golden)

To finish

1 tsp chopped coriander
1 tsp chopped mint

METHOD

In a heavy-bottomed pot, melt the vegetable ghee on low heat. Add the ginger-garlic paste and cook for a minute until fragrant. Drop in the cloves, cardamom, star anise, cinnamon, bay leaf and mace. Let them bloom gently in the ghee. Stir in the pilau spice mix. Let it toast for 30 seconds.

Add the drained rice and gently coat each grain in the spiced ghee. Pour in the water, salt, saffron water, rose water and fried onions. Stir once, gently. Bring to a boil on high. Once bubbles reach the surface, immediately reduce heat to low. Cover with a tight-fitting lid and cook for 12–14 minutes – no peeking.

Turn off the heat and let it rest for 5–8 minutes, lid still on. Then lift the lid and pick out any whole spices you can see. Use a flat spoon or spatula to gently fluff the rice without breaking the grains.

Finish with chopped coriander and mint just before serving.

Mission notes

Don't rush the resting stage – it's what gives you perfectly separate grains.

If your lid doesn't seal tightly, place a clean tea towel under it to catch moisture.

Want that restaurant-style finish? Dot the surface with a few drops of red or yellow food colouring before fluffing.

MORE
Thirsti times
Limcatimes
Limca
Limca
Limca
Limca
is veri veri lime'n' lemoni
6
උපසේන
හෙට්ටිආරච්චිට
6

TASTY
FAST FOOD CORN
SHOP NO.3/34. SAIFEE JUBILEE STR. MUMBAI-3.
OSK

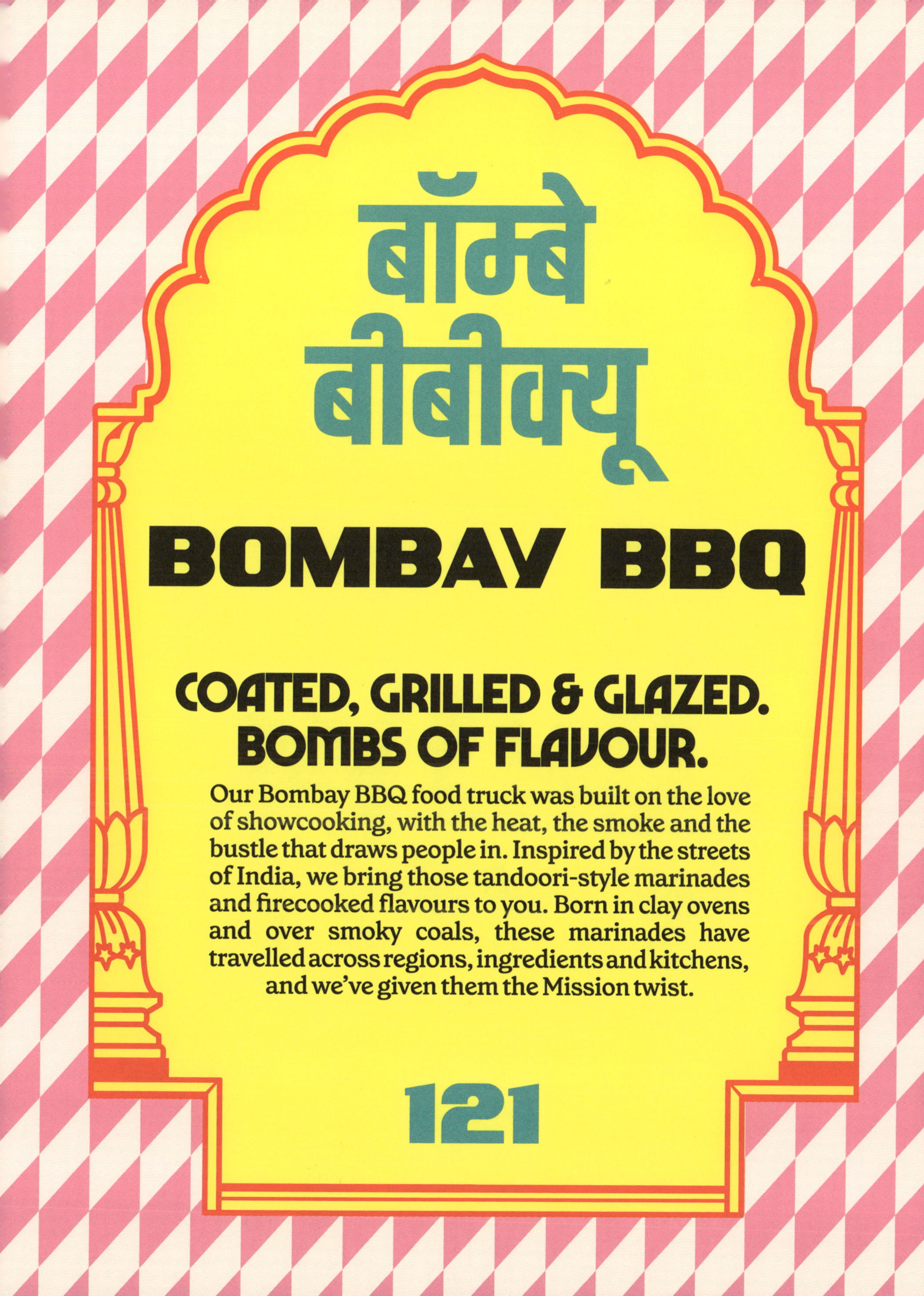

बॉम्बे बीबीक्यू

BOMBAY BBQ

COATED, GRILLED & GLAZED. BOMBS OF FLAVOUR.

Our Bombay BBQ food truck was built on the love of showcooking, with the heat, the smoke and the bustle that draws people in. Inspired by the streets of India, we bring those tandoori-style marinades and firecooked flavours to you. Born in clay ovens and over smoky coals, these marinades have travelled across regions, ingredients and kitchens, and we've given them the Mission twist.

PAAJI
INDIA PALE ALE

बीयर वाला
UMA
33CL
DESI BEER
BEER WALA

मास्टरक्लास
YOUR MARINADE MASTERCLASS

This is your starting point for bringing Mission Masala BBQ flavours into your kitchen, whether you are cooking in the oven, on the grill or over hot coals. Taste, adjust and make it your own.

BINDERS

The secret sauce behind every good marinade.

A binder makes the marinade stick, helps spices cling, keeps meat or veg juicy and adds flavour. In Indian cooking, hung yoghurt is a classic go-to for tenderness and tang, but the best binder depends on what you are cooking. There's no right way – just choose what suits the dish. But don't skip it because the binder brings it all together.

YOGHURT
creamy and classic, especially for chicken or lamb

GRAM FLOUR (BESAN)
nutty and light, great with veg or paneer

CREAM OR CHEESE
rich and indulgent, used in malai-style marinades

OIL OR MUSTARD OIL
sharp, smoky and essential for dry marinades

CASHEW OR NUT PASTES
smooth, luxurious and great for BBQs

FIRE & FLAVOUR TIPS

Marinate Like a Pro
Marinate for 2 to 4 hours, or overnight for deeper flavour.

•

Heat Matters
Preheat your grill or oven so it sears, locks in juices and adds smoky char.

•

Finish with Flair
Baste with butter, masala and warm marinade for a rich, glossy finish.

•

Zest It Up
Add lemon or lime juice or zest for fresh, bright flavour.

•

Sauce on the Side
Serve with chutney, mayo or gravy to bring it all together.

Marinades

OUR BIG 4

Your go-to marinade line-up. Each one does its own thing – and together, they cover just about everything you'd want to throw on a grill, bake in an oven, or sizzle in a pan.

We've broken them down so you can mix them, tweak them and make them your own.

1
TANDOORI MARINADE
तंदूरी मरिनाशन

The classic. Spicy, smoky and full of bold North Indian flavour. Red chilli, garam masala, yoghurt – this one's the most popular and definitely a crowd-pleaser.

<u>Suggestions for marination:</u>
Chicken legs, Lamb neck fillets , cauliflower or carrots

2
MALAI MARINADE
मलाई मरिनाशन

Creamy, cheesy and deceptively mild. With green chilli and cardamom underneath, it's rich, juicy and absolutely addictive.

<u>Suggestions for marination:</u>
Boneless chicken thigh, mushrooms or broccoli

3
ACHAARI MARINADE
अचारी मरिनाशन

Tangy, punchy and totally pickle-inspired, with flavours like mustard oil, kalonji, ajwain and a sharp acidic bite. Especially good on fish, paneer or veg.

<u>Suggestions for marination:</u>
Paneer, asparagus & butternut squash

4
MASALA MARINADE
मसाला मरिनाशन

Our wildcard. Big flavours, no rules. Dry spice-forward, garlicky, customisable and great when you want a big impact without the yoghurt.

<u>Suggestions for marination:</u>
Prawns, mushrooms & pumpkin

1

2

3

4

तंदूरी मरिनाशन

1. TANDOORI MARINADE

Smoky, spicy and full of bold North Indian flavour, this tandoori classic is our signature. Made with red chilli, garam masala and yoghurt, it's a crowd-pleaser that works just as well with meats as it does with veg and is easy to adapt to whatever you're cooking.

INGREDIENTS **marinates 500 g protein or veg**

1½ tbsp garlic-ginger paste
1 tsp Kashmiri red chilli powder (for colour)
½ tsp red chilli powder (for heat – adjust to taste)
1 tsp cumin powder
1 tsp coriander powder
½ tsp garam masala
½ tsp chaat masala
½ tsp dry ginger powder
½ tsp turmeric
1 tbsp kasuri methi (crushed between your palms)
½ tsp black salt
1 tsp salt (or to taste)
a small handful of finely chopped fresh coriander
1 tbsp lemon juice
1 tbsp mustard oil (it's a must for the flavour – can substitute a veg oil)

100 g yoghurt for chicken or lamb
OR
1 tbsp gram flour (besan) for paneer, mushrooms, potatoes or other veg

METHOD

Mix the garlic-ginger paste, spices, coriander, salts, lemon juice and oil into a thick paste.

In a mixing bowl, add yoghurt or gram flour, depending on what you are marinating and fold in the rest of the marination mix, until smooth and well combined.

Rub it all over your protein or veg. Really get in there and coat every bit. Cover and marinate for at least 2 hours (or overnight for even deeper flavour).

Mission notes

Want a hit of smoke? Add ¼ tsp smoked paprika.

If you're not using yoghurt, up the oil slightly to keep it moist.

मलाई मरिनाशन

2. MALAI MARINADE

Creamy and cheesy with a gentle kick, this is India's take on béchamel, turned up a notch. Green chilli and cardamom add heat and aroma to balance the richness. Perfect for juicy, smoky bites, malai (*cream*) comes alive in the blend of cream, cheese, and yoghurt, while cashews give body and help the marinade cling to your skewers.

INGREDIENTS **marinates 500 g protein**

Base
100 ml double cream
50 g grated cheddar cheese
90 g hung yoghurt (or 180 g full-fat yoghurt before straining)

Cashew & green chilli paste
25 g cashew nuts (soaked in warm water for 15–20 minutes)
10 g green chillies (de-stemmed)

Spices & aromatics
40 g ginger-garlic paste
½ tsp cumin powder
½ tsp garam masala
¼ tsp cardamom powder
10 g chopped fresh coriander
½ tsp salt (or to taste)

METHOD

Start by gently warming the cream in a small pan – don't let it boil. Once warm, stir in the grated cheddar and let it melt fully until you have a smooth, glossy mixture.

In a blender, blitz the soaked cashews and green chillies along with a splash of water into a smooth paste.

In a mixing bowl, combine the melted cheese-cream mix, hung yoghurt and the cashew-green chilli paste. Add the ginger-garlic paste, all the dry spices, chopped coriander and salt. Whisk it all together until creamy and well combined. Taste and tweak – it should be rich, salty and lightly spiced.

Coat your protein or veg thoroughly. Cover and chill for at least 2 hours (for meats, overnight is even better; veg can be pre-steamed, cooled and marinated).

This marinade is delicate, so avoid high, direct heat straight away. Let it caramelise gently for golden, charred edges.

KAR
rk of Quality
Marque de Qualité
DIAN TASTE / GR
DIEN
GREA

अचारी मरिनाशन

3. ACHAARI MARINADE

Powered by mustard oil and high on pickle spices and yoghurt, it's got punch and depth. Grill it hard for smoky charred edges and balance it out with something creamy or sweet on the side.

INGREDIENTS **marinates 500 g protein**

1½ tbsp mustard oil
½ tsp fennel seeds
½ tsp nigella seeds
½ tsp fenugreek seeds
½ tsp cumin seeds
½ tsp mustard seeds
100 g Greek yoghurt (full-fat)
1 tbsp lemon juice
1 tbsp ginger-garlic paste
1 tsp Kashmiri chilli powder
½ tsp turmeric
½ tsp roasted cumin powder
½ tsp dried mango powder
1 tsp salt, or to taste
1 tbsp chopped mixed veg pickle – (find your local Indian grocery and buy a jar of Indian mixed pickle)
1 fresh green chilli, finely chopped (optional)

METHOD

Start by heating the mustard oil in a small pan until it just begins to smoke. Switch off the heat and let it cool completely before using. This step softens the raw pungency and releases that unmistakable achar aroma – it's essential.

Toast all your whole seeds (fennel, nigella, fenugreek, cumin, mustard) in a dry pan until they smell warm and nutty. Let them cool, then crush coarsely with a mortar and pestle or spice grinder.

In a mixing bowl, combine the yoghurt, cooled mustard oil, lemon juice and ginger-garlic paste. Add the toasted crushed seed mix, all the ground spices and salt. Stir well until smooth. Mix in the chopped pickle or green chilli. If your chopped pickle is salty or spicy, adjust the rest of the seasoning accordingly.

Add your protein or veg of choice and coat it thoroughly in the marinade. Cover and refrigerate for at least 4 hours, or overnight for maximum depth.

Grill or roast on high heat until well charred and cooked through. Flip halfway and baste with ghee or butter if you want a richer finish.

Once off the heat, brush with more ghee or mustard oil, a fresh squeeze of lemon juice and a light dusting of extra pickle masala or crushed seeds if you want a bold, layered finish.

मसाला मरिनाशन

4. MASALA MARINADE

Your ace-in-the-hole – a bold, yoghurt-free spice rub that delivers serious depth. Built on oil, ginger-garlic paste and dry spices, this one gives you that deep colour and toasted masala crust.

INGREDIENTS **marinates 500 g protein**

2 tbsp mustard oil
1 heaped tbsp ginger-garlic paste
1 tsp turmeric
1 tbsp lemon juice
½ tsp cumin powder
¼ tsp coriander powder
½ tsp chilli powder (adjust to heat preference)
¾ tsp salt (can always add extra salt after cooking)

Optional extras

½ tsp garam masala
½ tsp chaat masala
½ tsp kasoori methi, crushed

METHOD

In a bowl, combine the oil and ginger-garlic paste. Add all the dry spices and salt. Stir together until you have a thick marinade that coats and clings.

Add lemon juice, kasoori methi, or any extras if using. Taste it – it should be bold and a little salty.

Massage into your protein or veg and let it marinate for at least 2 hours, or overnight if you've got the time.

Grill, roast or pan-fry over high heat until charred and cooked through. Baste with oil or butter as you go.

Mission notes

Anything made with this marination pairs well with a creamy mayo dip, tangy chutney or a crisp fresh salad. You can also use a spoon of the marinade to dress your salad.

Anything that comes off the BBQ, grill or oven MUST be buttered and seasoned again. That's how we build flavours at Mission Masala: layer by layer, bite by bite. We don't just season once and call it done; seasoning at every stage is non-negotiable. These butters bring the final boost of richness, heat and aroma that turn good dishes into unforgettable ones. Slather, melt and watch the magic happen.

Whether slathered on grilled meats, stirred into steamy rice, or melting over fresh bread, the butters we give you here deliver bold spice, fragrant warmth and a splash of indulgence.

You can also replace the butter with any plant-based alternative.

फ्लेवरर्ड बटर
FLAVOURED BUTTERS

BUTTERS THAT BRING THE HEAT & HEART

SMOKED CURRY BUTTER
स्मोक्ड करी बटर

Golden, rich and smoky, this one adds an instant hit of depth to anything from roast veg to BBQ meats.

INGREDIENTS

- 100 g unsalted butter, softened
- ½ tsp roasted cumin powder
- ½ tsp Kashmiri chilli powder (chilli flakes if you want bite)
- 1 tsp pink Himalayan salt
- 1 small piece of natural lump coal
- 1 tsp ghee

METHOD

Fire up the coal

Using tongs, heat the charcoal directly with an open flame (gas burner or blowtorch) until glowing red.

Set up for smoke

Place softened butter in a bowl and spread it flat for more smoke contact. Set a small steel or foil bowl in the centre, making sure it does not touch the butter to avoid melting.

Smoke

Carefully drop the hot coal into the steel bowl and pour over 1 tsp ghee – thick smoke will release instantly. Quickly cover with a tight lid or cling film and leave for 6–8 minutes.

Mash & mix

If the butter has melted slightly, refrigerate until it returns to a soft but firm stage. Then mix in cumin, chilli powder (if using) and salt until well combined.

Finish & store

Stir gently and transfer to a container. Refrigerate until firm.

Mission notes

Use this to finish anything off your BBQ or grill, stir into daal, or brush over hot naan straight out of the oven.

You can also roll it into a log, wrap in parchment and slice off discs as needed.

Want more funk? Add a pinch of black salt or a touch of crushed garlic before smoking.

ROASTED SEEDS & TURMERIC BUTTER
रोस्टेड सीड्स & टर्मेरिक

Warm Indian spice in a toasty, earthy and vibrant spreadable form. This butter's got range: rub it over roasted cauliflower, melt it over baked sweet potatoes, try a dab on your breakfast egg, on corn on the cob, or drop a spoonful into hot rice.

INGREDIENTS

- 100 g unsalted butter, softened

Dry roasted & crushed:

- 1 tsp cumin seeds
- ½ tsp coriander seeds
- ½ tsp fennel seeds
- ½ tsp black peppercorns
- ½ tsp turmeric powder
- zest of ½ lemon
- 1 tsp pink Himalayan salt
- 1 small garlic clove, grated or mashed (can also dry-roast with skin on with the seeds)

METHOD

Toast whole spices

In a dry pan, toast cumin, coriander, fennel seeds and black peppercorn for 1 minute on medium heat until fragrant and slightly darkened. Let cool slightly, then crush roughly using a mortar and pestle.

Mash & mix

In a bowl, combine the softened butter with crushed spices, turmeric, lemon zest and garlic. Mix well until fully combined and golden.

Shape or store

Spoon into a ramekin or roll into a log using parchment paper. Chill until firm.

GARLIC, CHILLI, CORIANDER & LIME BUTTER

गार्लिक, चिल्ली, कोरिएंडर & लाइम

Fresh, zingy and bright, this one gives any dish a hit of green heat and citrusy lift.

INGREDIENTS

2–3 garlic cloves, grated or finely chopped
½ fresh green chilli, finely chopped (or to taste)
2 tbsp fresh coriander, finely chopped
100 g unsalted butter, softened
1 tsp red chilli flakes
½ tsp Deggi mirch or smoked paprika
½ tsp black salt
1 tsp pink Himalayan salt
zest of 1 lime
squeeze of lime juice
cracked black pepper (optional)

METHOD

Grate & chop

Prep your garlic, green chilli and coriander. Zest the lime and squeeze in a little juice – just enough to brighten without making the butter too soft.

Mix it up

In a bowl, combine everything with the softened butter. Mix well until smooth and flecked with green herbs and red chilli.

Shape & chill

Spoon into a ramekin or roll into a log with parchment paper. Chill until firm. Slice or scoop as needed.

लांब सीख कबाब काठी रोल

LAMB SEEKH KEBAB KATHI ROLL

serves 6

Juicy lamb seekhs loaded with ginger, garlic and dried methi, grilled until golden and smoky, then wrapped in a buttery paratha that's fried into an eggy base. Layered with a fresh, spiced onion salad and Mission's signature chutneys, it's got heat, tang and comfort.

INGREDIENTS

For the kebabs

600 g minced lamb
15 g chopped coriander
15 g ground ginger
20 g ground garlic
2 g Deggi mirch
4½ g cumin powder
2½ g garam masala
3 g dried methi, crushed by rubbing in the palm of your hands
1 small green chilli, finely chopped
1 tsp salt (adjust if pre-seasoned)
1 tbsp melted ghee or fat (for brushing)

For the onion filling

2 small red onions, finely sliced
1 small bunch coriander, roughly chopped
juice of ½ lemon
½ tsp Deggi mirch
1 tsp chaat masala
salt to taste

For the roll

6 small eggs
6 plain parathas (see page 43 or use store-bought wraps or frozen parathas)

butter for the pan
salt & pepper for seasoning

To serve

coriander & mint chutney (see page 31)
tamarind chutney (see page 28)

METHOD

Start with the kebabs

In a large bowl, mix all kebab ingredients thoroughly by hand until the mixture is sticky and well combined. Rest in the fridge for at least 30 minutes so it firms up and binds. Don't leave it out. It's what helps them hold shape on the grill.

Shape into 6 tight sausage-like kebabs, around 100 g each. Skewer if using metal rods, or shape by hand for the pan or oven.

To cook:

BBQ: Grill over medium-high heat, turning often until golden and cooked through (8–10 minutes).
Grill: Cook under a hot oven grill, flipping halfway.
Pan: Sear in a hot cast-iron or non-stick pan until browned all over.

Brush with melted ghee or fat when done.

Now prep the onion salad filling

In a bowl, toss together sliced onions, coriander, lemon juice, Deggi mirch, chaat masala and salt. Set aside. This filling will add freshness and tang to cut through the richness of the kebab.

Make the paratha base

Whisk one egg per paratha with salt and pepper. In a hot pan, melt a little butter, pour in the egg, then press the cooked paratha directly on top. Let the egg set and stick, then flip and cook the other side until crisp and golden. Repeat with the rest. Keep warm.

Build the roll

Egg-side up, layer each paratha with a handful of onion salad, one hot lamb seekh, a drizzle of coriander & mint chutney and tamarind chutney. Roll tightly and serve hot.

Mission notes

Switch out the lamb mince for chicken, beef or pork mince.

For a spicier version, add green chilli to the onion salad or chutneys.

मलाई चिकन टोएस्टीज

MALAI CHICKEN TOASTIES

serves 4

An Indian-style Philly toastie stuffed with juicy malai-marinated chicken, melted cheese and our green chutney. Crispy on the outside, creamy, spicy and indulgent inside. Serve it hot with a sharp, herby kachumber to cut through all the richness. It's naughty and perfect.

INGREDIENTS

For the chicken:

400 g boneless skinless chicken thighs
100 g malai marinade (see page 126)
1 tbsp neutral oil

To finish the chicken

100 g reserved malai marinade
1 tbsp garlic, chilli, coriander & lime butter (see page 131)
½ tsp chaat masala

For the toastie

8 slices white sandwich bread (or sourdough if you're feeling fancy)
4 tbsp green chutney (see page 31)
120 g grated cheese (cheddar or mozzarella, or a mix)
garlic, chilli, coriander & lime butter for spreading

For the kachumber

½ small red onion, finely sliced
1 small bunch coriander, chopped
a few mint leaves, shredded
½ green chilli, finely chopped (optional)
juice of ½ lemon
pinch of Deggi mirch
sprinkle of chaat masala
¼ tsp Himalayan pink salt

METHOD

To cook the chicken:

BBQ: Grill on medium-high coals, flipping once, until lightly charred and cooked through (approx. 4–5 minutes per side).
Oven: Roast at 220°C (fan) on a wire rack over a tray for 12–15 minutes, or until golden with a few crispy edges.
Stovetop: Heat oil in a grill pan or skillet and fry the chicken until golden and fully cooked.

Toss the cooked chicken in a bowl with chaat masala and the spiced butter. Rest for a couple of minutes, then slice or shred.

In a separate pan, gently heat the reserved 100 g of malai marinade with a knob of butter and a pinch of chaat masala. Toss the grilled chicken back into this warm mix for a final coat of richness.

For the kachumber, toss all the ingredients together and chill until serving.

Butter the outside of your sandwich slices. Spread green chutney on the inside, layer with cheesy malai chicken, top with grated cheese, a handfull of kachumber and close the sandwich.

Toast in a sandwich press or hot pan until crisp and golden.

Mission notes

For a veg version: try this with grilled paneer, mushroom or jackfruit.

Feel free to throw in some chopped pickled green chillies.

तंदूरी चिकन नान
TANDOORI CHICKEN NAANWICH

makes 4

Grilled tandoori chicken stuffed into warm naan, topped with a tangy desi coleslaw, sharp red onion, fresh coriander and crispy Bombay mix. It's smoky, crunchy, creamy, messy and everything a proper naanwich should be.

INGREDIENTS

For the chicken

500 g chicken thigh marinated in tandoori marination (see page 126)
ghee to baste chicken
4 naan (see page 148)
butter, to brush the naan
80 g red onion, finely sliced
20 g fresh coriander, chopped
60 g Bombay mix
4 tbsp mango mayo (see page 29)
4 tbsp tamarind sauce (see page 28)
160 g desi coleslaw (see below)
A bag of Bombay mix or any crunchy Indian snack (see page 17)

For the desi coleslaw

100 g white cabbage, finely shredded
50 g carrot, grated or julienned
4 tbsp pickle dressing (see page 37 – use the tangy mustard oil one)
1 tsp chaat masala
½ tsp Deggi mirch
1 tsp toasted coriander and mustard seed
squeeze of lime

METHOD

To cook the tandoori chicken

Rest the chicken thighs at room temperature for 20 minutes before cooking.

BBQ: Grill over high heat for 5–6 minutes on each side until lightly charred and fully cooked through. Baste with mustard oil or ghee while grilling. Rest for 5 minutes before slicing.

Oven: Roast in a preheated oven at 220°C (fan) for 18–20 minutes, or until cooked through and starting to char. Finish under the grill for 2–3 minutes to add colour. Rest before slicing.

Stovetop: Heat a heavy pan or grill pan over medium-high heat. Add a little oil and cook the chicken 5–7 minutes per side until golden and fully cooked, pressing lightly to get a sear. Rest before slicing.

Slicing tip: Let the chicken rest before slicing so the juices stay in and the naan doesn't get soggy. Cut against the grain into thick strips or chunks.

To make the desi coleslaw

Make the coleslaw just before assembling – it keeps the veg crisp and stops the naan from going soggy.

In a bowl, combine shredded cabbage and carrot. Add the pickle dressing and toss well until everything is evenly coated. Let it sit for 10–15 minutes to slightly soften and absorb the dressing. Add chaat masala and a dusting of Deggi mirch if you want a little extra lift.

To assemble

Heat or toast the naan until soft and warm, then butter.

Lay down a generous smear of mango mayo.

Pile on sliced tandoori chicken, then top with a handful of desi coleslaw.

Add sliced red onion, chopped coriander and a drizzle of tamarind sauce.

Finish with a handful of crunchy Bombay mix just before serving.

Mission notes

Add green chutney if you want more heat, or a little pickle oil for extra kick.

गोअन प्रॉन्स मसाला

GOAN MASALA PRAWNS

serves 6

Tiger prawns, masala-marinated and fire-kissed. This is coastal BBQ done right, lightly spiced and perfectly charred. The marinade clings just enough to let the prawns shine. Serve straight off the grill with a lemon wedge or pile them onto the tangy, tamarind-spiked Tamil prawn curry on page 94.

INGREDIENTS

1.2 kg tiger prawns, shell-on or peeled (head-on optional)
masala marinade – 1x base recipe (for 500 g protein; see page 129)
lemon wedges, to serve
chaat masala, to finish
chopped coriander

METHOD

Pat the prawns dry and toss in the masala marinade. Use just enough to coat – you don't want it dripping. Keep a little bit of the marinade to heat baste the grilled prawns with later. Cover and marinate for 1–2 hours max.

When you are ready to cook the prawns, warm the reserved marinade with butter and brush over the prawns right after grilling.

BBQ: Grill over hot coals or on a BBQ rack for 2–3 minutes per side, just until the prawns are charred in spots and cooked through. Don't overdo it – they cook fast.

Oven: Roast on a wire rack in the oven at 220°C for 5–6 minutes.

Stovetop: Heat a heavy pan, add some butter and cook on high heat for 2–3 minutes per side.

Once off the heat, brush with warm marinade, squeeze over lemon, dust with chaat masala and scatter with chopped coriander.

Mission notes

Marinade works well with scallops, squid or even grilled baby aubergines.

तंदूरी सैल्मन टिक्का विद मैंगो सलाद

TANDOORI SALMON TIKKA WITH MANGO SALAD

serves 6

This dish is easy, soft and juicy. The salmon is coated in our signature tandoori marinade and grilled until charred outside, but juicy and tender on the inside. It's finished with a zingy mango salad that cuts through the richness, crunches and balances with the fattiness of the fish.

INGREDIENTS

For the salmon

6 skinless salmon fillets (around 180–200 g each), cut into chunky tikka-style pieces
tandoori marinade (from base recipe page 126)
lemon juice
chaat masala to dust
butter to baste

For the mango salad

1 firm green or very firm mango (julienned)
1 Persian cucumber (julienned with centre removed)
1 red banana pepper (finely sliced)
1–2 red chillies (thinly sliced)
handful of finely chopped coriander and mint
juice of ½ lime
1 tsp of mango chutney (see page 29)
pinch of salt and sugar
chaat masala to taste
Deggi mirch for dusting

METHOD

To cook the salmon

Lightly season salmon with salt and a squeeze of lemon. Coat generously with the tandoori marinade and chill for 1–2 hours max.

BBQ: Grill over medium-high heat for 2–3 minutes per side until just cooked and slightly charred.

Oven: Roast at 220°C on a wire rack for 8–10 minutes. Finish under the grill for extra colour if needed.

Stovetop: Sear on a hot grill pan with minimal oil until both sides are golden and the centre is just cooked.

Remove from the heat, baste with butter and dust with chaat masala.

Rest the fish for a couple of minutes and then sprinkle with lemon juice.

Prepare the mango salad

Prepare all ingredients and place them in a mixing bowl just before serving. Using your hands, gently mix and lightly bruise the mango, cucumber, pepper and herbs so the lime juice, chutney and spices coat everything evenly. This helps the dressing emulsify with the fresh ingredients. Taste and adjust the lime, salt and sugar to balance the flavours.

Mission notes

Mix the leftovers with mayo to put in a sandwich together with some watercress.

अचारी पनीर & वेज स्क्यूअर्स

makes 6

ACHAARI PANEER & VEG SKEWERS

Smoky, punchy and spiced like your favourite achaar, this dish pairs juicy button mushrooms with soft, grilled paneer for the perfect balance of charred edges, deep flavour and satisfying texture. A fun way to pimp up any veg.

INGREDIENTS

600 g paneer, cut into cubes of approximately 2½–3 cm
250 g button mushrooms, wiped clean, stems trimmed
150 g red onion, cut into thick petals
300 g achaari marinade (see page 129)
1 tsp besan flour – dry-roasted (optional, only if needed to bind)
ghee or butter to baste
chaat masala to dust

METHOD

Prep the veg

Clean mushrooms with a damp cloth – avoid washing them under water. If they feel damp, leave them to air-dry on a tray for 30–60 minutes.

Marinate

In a large bowl, combine the paneer, mushrooms and red onion. Add the achari marinade and toss gently until everything is coated evenly.

If needed, add 1 tsp roasted besan to help the marinade cling, especially if moisture was released during prep. If your marinade is thick and the veg are dry, besan is usually not needed. Only add it if the marinade looks loose after tossing.

Thread the veg and paneer onto skewers, alternating pieces for colour and texture. Aim for even spacing to allow the heat to circulate.

Cover and marinate in the fridge for 2–4 hours.

Grill immediately after removing from the fridge.

To cook

BBQ: Grill the skewers over high direct heat until lightly charred on all sides, turning every few minutes. Baste with mustard oil, ghee or butter during cooking to prevent drying and to deepen flavour. Total cooking time: around 10–12 minutes depending on the heat. (The marinade may stick to the grill; you can use a wire rack to reduce the chances of this.)

Oven: Preheat oven to 220°C (fan). Place skewers on a lined baking tray or wire rack and roast for 15–18 minutes, turning once halfway through. For best results, finish under the grill (broiler) for 2–3 minutes to get that charred finish. Baste mid-way through with ghee or oil.

Stovetop: Heat a grill pan or cast-iron griddle over medium-high heat. Lightly oil the pan. Place the skewers in a single layer and cook for 10–12 minutes, turning every 2–3 minutes to ensure even colouring. Press gently to get a sear. Baste with ghee or butter as they cook.

Remove from heat, baste with more butter and dust with chaat masala. Serve in a wrap (naan or paratha), with a salad, or simply drizzled with your favourite sauce or chutney.

Mission notes

The drier the veg, the better the char and cling.

Watery vegetables like mushrooms can release moisture during cooking – this causes the marinade to slide off and steam instead of char. To avoid that, always salt and dry veg first, or lightly roast watery veg before mixing into the marinade.

Veg alternatives

Use the same technique when working with high-moisture or dense veg. Here are some top picks that work beautifully with achaari marinade:
Fennel – cut into thin wedges, grills up sweet and aromatic.
Cauliflower – parboil florets until just tender before marinating.
Celeriac – dice and steam or roast lightly before adding.

मसाला पनीर स्टफ्ड पैड्रोन पेपर्स

MASALA PANEER STUFFED PADRON PEPPERS

serves 6

Charred padron peppers stuffed with paneer and cheddar, finished with a sprinkle of Maldon. This might not be a traditional dish, but the technique of stuffing vegetables with seasoned paneer is a long-standing favourite in Indian cooking.

INGREDIENTS

30 padron peppers
2 tbsp smoked curry butter (optional)
Maldon salt

For the stuffing

300 g grated paneer
300 g grated mozzarella
25 g chopped coriander
30 g roasted cumin powder
1 tbsp chaat masala
1 chopped green chilli (add more if you like the heat)
cotton thread to tie around the peppers

To serve

curry leaf tartare (see page 34)

METHOD

Mix all the stuffing ingredients in a bowl. It should be a loose but scoopable mix.

Slit each padron pepper lengthwise down one side. Gently remove the seeds with a small spoon or the back of a knife, but be careful not to tear them. If they are too difficult to handle when stuffed, roll a bit of cotton thread around them so the stuffing doesn't fall out when cooking.

Stuff each pepper generously with the cheese mixture and lay them on a tray.

Chill in the fridge for 15–20 minutes to help the filling set.

Melt the butter if using.

To cook:

BBQ: Grill over hot coals, turning occasionally, until the skins are blistered and the cheese is soft and melty – around 3–5 minutes total depending on heat.
Grill: Place under a hot oven grill, turning once, until the peppers are blistered and the cheese is cooked through.
Stovetop: In a cast-iron or grill pan, sear on high heat until charred on all sides. Handle carefully so the stuffing doesn't fall out.

Remove from the heat and cut off the threads; brush with smoked curry butter if using.

To plate, place 5 grilled peppers per portion, sprinkle with crushed Maldon salt. Serve with a dollop of curry leaf tartare to dip.

Mission notes

Experiment with different stuffings, like tempered garlic mushroom with similar spices.

Leftover stuffing? Use it in naan toasties, parathas, or as a stuffing for mushrooms.

अचारी ऐस्पैरागस

ACHAARI ASPARAGUS

makes 6

Not your typical BBQ veg, but once you've tried asparagus with a hit of achaari spice and that smoky char, you'll be blown away by what you've been missing. Grilled hot and fast, then tossed in our masala-pickle marinade and finished with creamy achaari mayo and coconut sambol from the Sauces, Chutneys & Condiments section, they are tangy, crunchy and totally unexpected. The sambol adds bite and texture, so be sure not to skip it.

INGREDIENTS

18–20 asparagus spears, trimmed
achaari marinade (see page 129 – make a version without yoghurt)
neutral oil for grilling
Maldon salt or sea salt
2 tbsp smoked curry butter (see page 130)
chaat masala for dusting

For the achaari mayo

150 g Greek-style yoghurt
150 g plain mayonnaise
2 tbsp achaari marinade (without yoghurt)
1 tsp lemon juice

To serve

coconut sambol (see page 35)
finely chopped coriander

Optional

sliced green chilli or a dusting of Deggi mirch

METHOD

Steam the asparagus for 1 minute until just softened. Pat dry and season with Maldon salt. Loosen a spoonful of the achaari marinade with a splash of oil and toss the asparagus in it.

Melt the curry butter and mix into the remaining marinade. Keep aside to baste asparagus once off the heat.

To make the mayo, mix the yoghurt, mayonnaise, lemon juice and achaari marinade in a small bowl until smooth.

To cook:

BBQ: Grill directly over hot coals, turning every minute or so until charred and just tender, around 4–5 minutes.
Grill: Place under a hot oven grill, turning once, until blistered and golden.
Stovetop: In a cast-iron or grill pan, sear on high heat until charred on all sides.

Remove from heat and toss back into a bowl with the melted butter mix.

Plate the asparagus with a generous spoonful of achaari mayo as the base, top with asparagus, and drizzle a scoop of coconut sambol on top. Finish with chopped coriander or sliced green chilli.

Mission notes

Serve this as a side or let it stand on its own with a cold beer or lassi.

This also works great with tenderstem broccoli, okra or grilled courgette.

Avoid over-marinating – you want char, not soggy stalks.

Since you're making the achaari mayo anyway, why not double the recipe so you can also use it in burgers or wraps?

सॉफ्ट & पफी नान

SOFT & PUFFY NAAN THREE WAYS

makes 8 naans

Fluffy, golden and blistered just right — naan is the ultimate curry sidekick. Here's a no-nonsense recipe for soft pan-cooked naan, plus three simple ways to switch it up: plain, garlic and cheese & onion.

INGREDIENTS

For the base naan dough

- 150 ml warm water
- 1 tsp sugar
- 5 g active dry yeast
- 500 g all-purpose flour
- ½ cup plain yoghurt
- ¾ tsp salt
- 1 tbsp neutral oil (plus more for cooking)
- 3 tbsp melted butter (to finish)

METHOD

Whisk the sugar into the warm water and sprinkle the yeast over the top. Let sit for 10 minutes until foamy.

In a bowl or directly on your work surface, combine the flour, yoghurt, salt, oil and the activated yeast mixture. Mix until it comes together, then knead for 8–10 minutes until smooth and elastic.

Lightly oil the dough, cover and leave to rise for 1 hour or until doubled in size.

Punch down and divide into 8 equal pieces. Roll each into a ball, then roll out into 20 cm ovals (about ½ cm thick).

Heat a dry cast-iron pan or heavy skillet until very hot. Cook each naan for 1–2 minutes per side until puffed and blistered. Brush with melted butter and keep wrapped in a clean cloth.

Mission notes

Use yoghurt for that soft, pillowy texture and light tang.

If your yeast is sluggish, add a pinch of baking powder.

These freeze well — just reheat in a dry pan or oven.

Best served hot with lots of butter and something saucy.

VARIATIONS

1. PLAIN NAAN
प्लाइन नान

Simply cook according to the recipe and finish with butter. Try sprinkling with nigella seeds or sesame seeds before cooking for extra texture.

2. GARLIC NAAN
गार्लिक नान

Before cooking, press a little minced garlic and chopped coriander onto one side of the rolled dough. Cook garlic-side down first. Finish with garlic butter for more punch.

3. CHEESE & ONION NAAN
चीज़ & अनयिन नान

Mix 75 g of grated cheddar with ¼ of a red onion, finely chopped. Place 1 tbsp of filling in the centre of the rolled-out dough. Fold the edges over, pinch to seal, then gently roll again to flatten. Cook as usual, flipping carefully.

ज्योति
ब्रांड
सरसों तेल
गोयल उद्योग
नमस्कार
दुनिया
बॉम्बे बारबेक्यु
टेम्पल दाँत घर
R.N. Mukherjee
सुभो
सिमेन्ट
TOILETS
शौचालय

R RALSON
रालसन
टायर • ट्यूब • हब
LIQUOR STOR
अंग्रेजी
ALL NATURAL WINE WHISKY RUM VODKA GIN
COLD LASSI 15/-
ROSE LASSI 15/-
MIX LASSI 25/-
TEA
COFFEE
DHOLAK
अंग्रेजी
नगर निगम, वाराणसी
वार्ड-भेलूपुर
B.4/65
मो. अवधसर्की

देस्सेर्ट्स

DESSERTS

STICKY, KITSCH & UNAPOLOGETICALLY SWEET(ISH).

We'll be honest, desserts aren't really our zone. But some things just belong at the table, and a sweet ending is one of them. So, we've added a few classics, given them a Mission twist, and turned the sugar down (just a bit) for those of us who didn't grow up on syrup-soaked everything.

No pastry cheffing here, just fun, nostalgic flavours, easy wins and a few cool-down moments after all the spice.

रोज & कार्डामम कुल्फी

ROSE & CARDAMOM KULFI

makes 16

A no-churn, frozen Indian classic, creamy and perfumed with rose and cardamom. This version is simple to make and sets in a silicone mould.

INGREDIENTS
350 g sugar
900 g unsweetened condensed milk
10 g cardamom powder
10 g rose water
1 litre full-fat (40%) fresh cream

For the garnish
chopped pistachio
rose petals

METHOD

In a large bowl, whisk together the sugar, condensed milk, cardamom powder, rose water and cream until the sugar fully dissolves. The mixture should be smooth and well combined.

Pour into sections of your silicone mould, filling each cavity evenly. You can set it in any mould you like, just make sure it's easy to pop out once frozen. Gently top with rose petals and pistachios. If they fall through the kulfis, leave the moulds in the freezer for an hour or so and go back to top them.

Freeze for at least 6 hours, or until completely set.

To serve, briefly dip the mould in warm water to loosen, then unmould the kulfi.

Mission notes

Kulfi is denser than ice cream and melts slower, so it's perfect for warm weather. The rose gives a floral lift while the cardamom adds gentle spice.

Storage tip

Keep the kulfis covered in the mould or transfer unmoulded kulfis to an airtight container.

गुलाब जामुन

makes 20

GULAB JAMUN

Golden, syrup-soaked dumplings made from milk solids. A sort of Desi Indian doughnut, they are soft, spongy and perfumed with rose, cardamom and chai spices. This small-batch version makes around 20 jamuns, perfect for family or a dinner party.

INGREDIENTS

For the sugar syrup

250 g sugar
280 ml water
1 cardamom pod, lightly crushed
1 small piece cassia bark (about 3 g)
1 clove
pinch star anise (⅛ tsp, optional)
1 tsp rose water

For the jamun dough

135 g full-fat milk powder (TRS)*
25 g all-purpose flour
22 g fine semolina (TRS)*
pinch baking soda (⅛ tsp)
pinch cardamom powder (⅛ tsp)
warm milk, as needed, to make a smooth dough

ghee or neutral oil, for frying

** I have included the brand name of the milk powder and semolina here because texture can vary between brands.*

METHOD

Make the syrup by simmering sugar, water, cardamom, cassia, clove and star anise for about 5 minutes until lightly sticky. Stir in the rose water and keep warm on very low heat.

Mix milk powder, flour, semolina, baking soda and cardamom powder. Add warm milk gradually until you have a soft, smooth dough. Rest, covered, for 10 minutes.

Divide the dough into about 20 small equal portions and roll into smooth balls with no cracks. If the balls crack, add a few drops more milk.

Heat ghee or oil on low-medium, around 150–160°C. Fry jamuns in batches, stirring gently, until evenly deep golden brown.

Drop straight into the warm syrup and let soak for at least two hours before serving. Overnight is best. Always soak while the syrup is warm, not boiling. Serve warm, garnished with pistachios or saffron if you like.

Mark of Quali
Marque de Qual
REAT INDIAN TASTE / GRANDE GOÛT INDIEN
AN SNACKS / COLLAT S INDENNES
Packed & E
THAKAR TS
SNACKS / COLLATIONS

ग्रिल्ड रम पाइनएप्पल & कोकोनट कुल्फी

GRILLED RUM PINEAPPLE & COCONUT KULFI

serves 6

Juicy pineapple wedges soaked in spiced rum syrup, oven-roasted until caramelised, and served with rich, creamy coconut kulfi. Finished with a glossy, reduced rum syrup and toasted coconut shavings. This is the perfect excuse to pull out a bottle of Mission Masala's pineapple rum. Works equally well with mango, peaches or even grilled bananas.

INGREDIENTS

For the rum syrup

250 ml water
60 ml dark rum
pinch saffron (about 0.2 g)
1 blade mace
1 green cardamom pod
1 small star anise
40 g sugar

For the pineapple

1 ripe pineapple, peeled, cored and cut into 12 wedges

For the thickened coconut kulfi

400 ml coconut milk
200 ml double cream
200 g unsweetened condensed milk
80 g caster sugar
1 tsp cardamom powder
30 g desiccated coconut, lightly toasted

To serve

2 tbsp toasted coconut shavings

METHOD

Make the rum syrup by combining water, rum, saffron, mace, cardamom, star anise and sugar in a small pot. Bring to a boil, then simmer gently for 10–12 minutes until fragrant. Remove from heat and allow to cool completely.

Place pineapple wedges in a shallow dish and pour over the cooled rum syrup. Cover and chill for at least 2 hours, turning halfway, so the pineapple absorbs the flavours.

Prepare the kulfi. In a heavy-bottomed saucepan, combine coconut milk, cream, condensed milk, sugar and cardamom powder. Simmer gently over medium heat, stirring frequently, until the mixture thickens slightly (coats the back of a spoon, about 10–15 minutes). Remove from heat and stir in the toasted desiccated coconut. Let cool to room temperature. Pour into kulfi moulds and freeze for at least 8 hours, preferably overnight.

Roast the pineapple in a preheated oven at 120°C. Remove pineapple wedges from the syrup, letting excess drip off. Place on a lined baking tray and roast for 20 minutes until caramelised and fragrant. Set aside.

To make the reduced syrup, take 2–3 tbsp of the leftover rum syrup and simmer gently in a small pan until it thickens slightly to a glaze consistency.

Heat your griddle pan and butter lightly or use a BBQ, place the pineapple on the heat and char to get some beautiful grill marks. Cook 2–3 minutes on each side and they're ready.

To serve, place two pineapple wedges on each plate. Unmould a scoop of coconut kulfi alongside. Drizzle with the reduced rum syrup and sprinkle with toasted coconut shavings.

Mission notes

Keep the kulfi frozen until ready to serve.

Pineapple can be pre-soaked in the syrup and roasted ahead of time; store covered in the fridge.

Assemble just before serving for the best presentation and flavour.

फंकी फलूदा

serves 6–8

FUNKY FALOODA

Falooda is all about drama, served in a tall glass to show the colourful layers. A party in a glass, the ultimate Indian summer dessert or drink. Creamy, floral and crunchy with layers of milk, rose-syrup-soaked noodles, basil seeds, pistachios, kulfi and a cherry on top.

INGREDIENTS

For the falooda milk
1 litre whole milk
305 ml condensed milk
1 tsp sugar

For the falooda sev
200 g falooda sev (vermicelli)
400 ml Rooh Afza rose syrup

For the basil seeds
10 g basil seeds
100 ml water

Other ingredients
50 g crushed pistachios
50 g rose & cardamom kulfi
(see page 154)
10 ml Rooh Afza syrup per glass
6–8 glacé cherries

METHOD

Heat the milk, condensed milk and sugar in a pot on low/medium heat. Stir gently until everything is dissolved and combined. Set aside to cool, then chill in the fridge.

Bring a pot of water to the boil and cook the noodles for about 5 minutes until just done. Drain and place in a container. Pour over the rose syrup and mix well. Refrigerate and let infuse for at least 24 hours.

Soak the seeds in water for at least 24 hours. Once they've swelled up into soft, jelly-like pearls, keep refrigerated until ready to use.

Assembly

Before serving, put 10 ml Rooh Afza syrup in the bottom of each sundae glass. Use a spoon to spread the syrup up from the base of the sundae glass to the tip of the rim; do this all the way around. Chill in freezer.

Add a scoop of rose-soaked noodles, a spoonful of basil seeds and a sprinkle of pistachios. Pour in 100 ml of the chilled falooda milk. Repeat the layering once more: noodles, basil seeds, pistachios, milk.

Finish with a scoop of kulfi and a glacé cherry on top. Serve immediately.

DHOLAK
चरम की
TANPURA
दुकान
GUITAR

ஜெ.பி.சௌத்ரி
J.B. CHOUDHARY
பாம்பே லஸ்ஸி
BOMBAY LASSI Rs 30.00
லஸ்ஸி ஐஸ் இல்லாமல் Rs 30.00
LASSI WITHOUT ICE Rs 35.00
தயிர் 1கிளாஸ் Rs 35.00
CURD 1GLASS Rs 35.00
Rs 35.00
NO EXTRA GLASS
ONE BY TWO NOT AVAILABLE

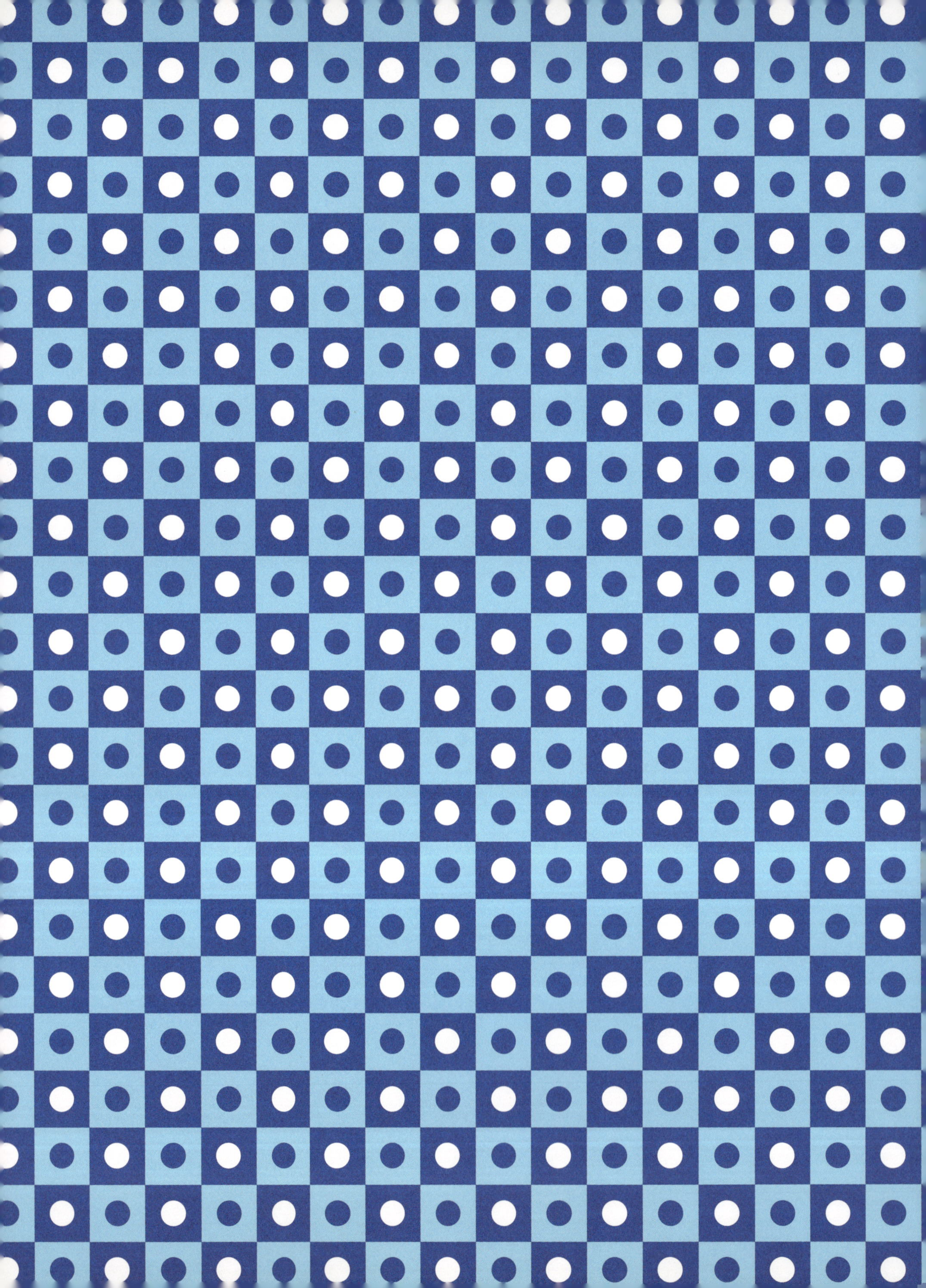

BOOZY MEETS BOLLYWOOD.

Classics with a twist. Give us anything and we can make it Indian. Whether you're winding down or turning up, these cocktails pack punch, flavour, and just the right amount of mischief. Let's get this party started...

TOOLS & RULES
BAR KIT BASICS

You don't need a full bar setup to get started, but a few good tools go a long way. These are the basics we reach for every time we shake something up. If you're missing one or two, it's no big deal – improvise or invest as you go.

Little Tips, Big Difference:
HOW TO NAIL YOUR COCKTAILS

The more ice, the better
Your drink will cool down faster and the ice will melt more slowly, keeping your drink undiluted for longer.

No need to stress over having the perfect glass. Use what you've got and keep it fun.

Got a sweet tooth?
Feel free to add a little extra sugar syrup.

Shaking
Dry shake as hard as you can to get a nice foam. If you're shaking with ice cubes, use a circular motion so the ice rotates instead of breaking – that helps avoid ice chips that dilute your drink.

Egg whites
1 egg gives you about 3 cl of egg white, perfect for one cocktail. Save the yolk for baking or use pre-separated egg whites.

A good vegan alternative is aquafaba (the liquid from a can of chickpeas).

Always sieve citrus juices
Pulp changes the texture of the cocktail. All measurements are without pulp.

Chill your glass
To chill your glass, fill it with crushed ice (making sure it touches all edges) and set aside while you're mixing the drink. Or, if you have the room, put your glasses in the freezer ahead of time.

Stirring
If the recipe specifies seconds of stirring, the stirring is meant to dilute and chill your drink. If not, the goal is just to gently blend the ingredients.

Double strain
Double strain means: place a strainer on the shaker and pour out the liquid, through a fine sieve, into the glass. Most shakers are big enough to make two cocktails at once.

BASIC TOOLS

SHAKER
For getting that proper chill and dilution.

JIGGER
Measuring = consistency. Eyeballing is fine... until it's not.

STRAINER
Keeps the ice (and any unwanted bits) out of your glass.

BAR SPOON
Long, lean, and made for stirring like a pro.

SMALL SIEVE
For that clean pour. Especially useful with citrus or egg whites.

CITRUS JUICER
Fresh juice hits different. Trust us.

BLENDER
Not essential, but great for frozen drinks or infusions.

RUM
OUR RIDE OR DIE

Rum is where the party starts. It's the soul of most cocktails in this chapter, and for good reason — we love the stuff. It's tropical, it's versatile, and it plays well with spice, citrus, fruit and heat.

At Mission, we work with two signature blends:

HOUSE BLEND RUM

A custom mix of tropical rums, smooth with just enough bite. Built to hold its own in anything from a punchy sour to a slow sipper.

If you can't get your hands on ours, go for something smooth so the base is easy to build on.

PINEAPPLE RUM

Infused in-house with real pineapple. Juicy, vibrant, and made to shine in anything bright and sunny.

If you can't get hold of a pineapple rum, the next best thing is to infuse it yourself, by cutting a few slices of pineapple and soaking them in the rum for a few days or just adding a splash of pineapple juice into the actual drink.

We always reach for tropical-style rums — they've got warmth, body and real character. If you can get your hands on our blends, use them. If not, go for a good spiced or golden rum with depth.

Flavour profile	serves	Glass
tropical/sweet	4	long drink

TIKKI PAAJI

A tropical tiki with a Mission twist – made extra special thanks to our very own Paaji beer. Bold, juicy and unapologetically fun.

INGREDIENTS

For the prep
120 ml spiced rum
120 ml gin
175 ml pineapple juice
25 ml ginger juice
60 ml lime juice
60 ml ginger syrup

To serve
ice cubes
5 cl Paaji beer (or any IPA beer)

Garnish
fresh or dehydrated lime and pineapple

METHOD

First, make the prep by combining the spirits, juices and syrup in a container. Chill in the fridge.

To serve

Pour 14 cl of the prep into a glass. Fill the glass with ice cubes. Top up with the beer. Give it a quick stir in gentle circular motions.

Garnish and serve.

BEER
PAAJI
DOUBLE DRY HOPPED
INDIA PALE ALE
33CL
7.5%

Flavour profile	serves	Glass
refreshing/juicy	4	long drink

मानसून मोजितो

MONSOON MOJITO

A tangy take on the classic mojito – just as refreshing, with an extra hit of bold, juicy flavour.

INGREDIENTS

For the prep
160 ml Mission Masala's house-blend rum
30 ml spiced syrup
60 ml lime juice
260 ml cranberry juice
100 ml pomegranate juice (unsweetened)

To serve
10 mint leaves
crushed ice
5 cl soda

Garnish
mint sprig & pomegranate arils

METHOD

First, make the prep by combining the spirits, juices and syrup in a container. Chill in the fridge.

To make one drink
In a glass, muddle the mint leaves and then add 15 cl of prep. Fill ¾ of the glass with crushed ice. Top with soda. Mix gently by stirring in circular motions.

Garnish and serve.

VIRGIN MONSOON MOJITO

INGREDIENTS

50 ml spiced syrup
100 ml lime juice
400 ml cranberry juice
150 ml pomegranate juice (unsweetened)

METHOD

For a non-alcoholic version, use these ingredients and follow the instructions to prepare the drink in the same way as the mojito.

Flavour profile	serves	Glass
creamy/tangy	4	tumbler

RUMBA SOUR

Our house-blend rum meets bold Assam tea and a citrusy lime leaf–honey syrup. Shaking with fresh lemon and egg whites gives it a smooth, creamy finish with just the right tang.

INGREDIENTS

For the prep
200 ml Mission Masala's house-blend rum
120 ml lemon juice
160 ml assam syrup (see below)

To serve
3 cl egg white (+/- white from 1 separated egg)
2 dashes aromatic bitters
ice cubes

Garnish
lime leaf

METHOD

First, make the prep by combining the rum, juice and syrup in a container. Chill in the fridge.

To serve

Grab your shaker! First, add the egg whites, bitters and 12 cl of the prep into a shaker tin and dry shake (without ice) for 10–15 seconds. Then fill the shaker with ice cubes and shake for another 10–15 seconds.

Fill the glass with 4 ice cubes and strain the cocktail into the glass over the ice.

Run the lime leaf around the rim of the glass and place the leaf on top. Serve.

ASSAM SYRUP

INGREDIENTS

200 ml honey syrup made with 65 ml honey + 135 ml water
5 g Assam tea
1 star anise

METHOD

Place all the ingredients in a pot and simmer on low heat (don't boil) for 15 minutes. Strain and cool.

KTHI FIREWORKS,

Flavour profile	serves	Glass
creamy/tropical	4	long drink

कोलकाता कोलाडा
KOLKATA COLADA

Creamy, tropical and unapologetically extra. Pineapple rum, spiced ginger liqueur, and our lush lime leaf coconut infusion come together in a frozen cocktail that brings sunshine to your glass.

INGREDIENTS

For the prep
150 ml Mission Masala's pineapple rum
100 ml spiced ginger liqueur
300 ml lime leaf coconut infusion (see below)
300 ml pineapple juice

To serve
lime juice
shredded coconut
a scoop of crushed ice

Garnish
umbrella with cherry, dehydrated pineapple, dehydrated lime, pineapple leaf, sprinkle of cinnamon powder... go wild with it! It's a tiki drink so be as kitschy and colourful as you like.

METHOD

First, make the prep by combining the spirits, juice and coconut infusion in a container. Chill in the fridge.

To make one drink

Rim the glass with lime juice and dip it into shredded coconut. Add 20 cl of prep and the crushed ice to a blender. Blend for 10 seconds. Pour everything into the glass.

Garnish and serve.

LIME LEAF COCONUT INFUSION

INGREDIENTS

200 ml coconut milk
200 ml coconut cream
10 frozen lime leaves

METHOD

Simmer on low heat for 20 minutes.

Strain and cool.

MISSION MASALA'S
PINEAPPLE

Flavour profile	serves	Glass
herby/floral	4	large water glass

जिन एंड टी

G & TEA

More than just a gin & tonic. This one's layered with citrus, botanicals, and florals from our Earl Grey-infused gin, spiced up with elderflower syrup and a splash of red vermouth. Fresh, fizzy, and anything but basic.

INGREDIENTS

For the prep
250 ml black tea gin (see below)
100 ml red vermouth
75 ml elderflower syrup (see below)
150 ml lime juice

To serve
crushed ice
5 cl tonic

Garnish
mint sprig, dehydrated lime

METHOD

First, make the prep by combining the gin, vermouth, syrup and juice in a container. Chill in the fridge.

To serve

Pour 12 cl of prep into a glass. Fill ¾ with crushed ice. Top with the tonic and stir gently.

Garnish and serve.

BLACK TEA GIN

Infuse ½ l of London dry gin with 10 g or 4 bags of black tea. Pour the gin into an airtight container and leave the tea bags to soak for 2 days.

Remove the tea bags and pour the gin back into a bottle.

ELDERFLOWER SYRUP

Combine 200 ml of simple syrup and 5 g of dried elderflowers in a pan.

Simmer on low heat for 20 minutes.

Remove and cool overnight. Strain and store the next day.

Flavour profile: sweet/elegant | *serves* 4 | Glass: chilled coupe

अलीची
ALYCHEE

A floral and fizzy explosion — lychee, rose, and a touch of lime topped with bubbles. If pink had a flavour, this would be it.

INGREDIENTS

For the prep
80 ml lychee liqueur
120 ml vodka
200 ml lychee juice
20 ml rose syrup (see next page)
60 ml rose water
40 ml lime juice

To serve
ice cubes
5 cl sparkling wine

Garnish
a few dried rose petals or a fresh lychee

METHOD

First, make the prep by combining the spirits, juices and syrup in a container. Chill in the fridge.

To make one drink

In a glass, muddle the mint leaves and then add 15 cl of prep. Fill ¾ of the glass with crushed ice. Top with soda. Mix gently by stirring in circular motions.

Garnish and serve.

VIRGIN ALYCHEE

INGREDIENTS

For the prep
350 ml lychee juice
35 ml rose syrup (see next page)
75 ml rose water
40 ml lime juice

To serve
ice cubes
10 cl soda

Garnish
mint sprig, dehydrated lime

METHOD

First, make the prep by combining the juices, syrup and rose water in a container. Chill in the fridge.

To make one drink

Add 11 cl of prep to a shaker filled with ice cubes. Stir for 15 seconds, then strain into a chilled coupe glass. Top with the soda and stir gently to mix.

Garnish and serve.

ROSE SYRUP

INGREDIENTS

200 ml simple syrup
10 g dried rose petals
5 ml rose water

METHOD

Place ingredients in a pan and simmer on low heat for 20 minutes. Cool, remove rose petals and store.

Flavour profile
fruity/punch style

serves
4

Glass
footed tumbler

मेज़कॉल मिर्ज़ा

MEZCAL MIRZA

A royal mezcal cocktail layered with tropical heat and smoky depth. Passion fruit, lime, habanero and a hint of sumac. Flavour on top of flavour exploding onto your palate.

INGREDIENTS

For the prep
300 ml mezcal
300 ml passion fruit purée
50 ml lime juice
200 ml habanero syrup (see below)
2 g sumac powder

To serve
lime
sumac powder
a scoop of crushed ice

Garnish
coriander leaf

METHOD

First, combine the prep ingredients in a container and chill in the fridge.

To make one drink

Rim ¼ of the glass with lime and sumac powder. Put 20 cl of prep and the crushed ice to a blender. Blend for 10 seconds and pour all the contents into the glass.

Garnish and serve.

HABANERO SYRUP

Start with 200 ml simple syrup, add ¼ habanero (seeds removed). Bring to a gentle boil and simmer for 5 minutes.

Taste – you're looking for spicy but not flaming hot.

If it's still too mild, add another ¼ habanero and simmer a few more minutes.

Strain and cool before using.

Flavour profile	serves	Glass
sweet/fruity	4	footed tumbler

मंगरीता

MANGORITA

Tropical margarita on the rocks with a serious kick. Tequila and mezcal blend with fresh mango, lime and spicy habanero syrup for a sweet, smoky and fiery finish.

INGREDIENTS

For the prep
160 ml tequila
80 ml mezcal
180 ml mango purée (from 2 sweet, peeled mangoes)
60 ml habanero syrup (see page 180)
120 ml lime juice

To serve
lime
tajín
ice cubes

Garnish
coriander leaf

METHOD

First, combine the prep ingredients in a container and chill in the fridge.

To make one drink

Rim the glass with lime and tajín spices. Fill the glass ¾ full with ice cubes. Add 15 cl prep to the glass. Stir gently for 15 seconds. Garnish and serve.

Flavour profile	*serves*	Glass
creamy/surprising	*4*	chilled low coupe

इंडियन एक्सप्रेस

INDIAN EXPRESS

Here we give the espresso martini the Mission treatment: bold coffee liqueur, smooth bourbon, fresh espresso and our homemade masala chai. Finished with grated salted dark chocolate and a touch of chilli powder. A great way to end your evening or get it started.

INGREDIENTS

For the prep
120 ml coffee liqueur (with chocolate notes)
120 ml bourbon
120 ml espresso
120 ml homemade chai (see page 188)

To serve
ice cubes

Garnish
half grated dark chocolate (70% cacao, salted), half chilli powder

METHOD

First, combine the prep ingredients in a container. Chill in the fridge.

To make one drink

Add 12 cl of the prep to a shaker filled with ice cubes. Shake for 12 seconds. Strain into a chilled low coupe.

Garnish and serve.

कूलर्स
COOLERS

You don't need booze to enjoy good drinks. Whether you're the designated driver or just skipping the hard stuff, we've got you. From classic chai and lassi to a tropical mix with tamarind – these drinks deliver big flavour with zero hangover.

Flavour profile	serves	Glass
milky/spiced/herby	4	teacup

MISSION MASALA CHAI

मिशन मसाला चाय

Sweet, milky and deeply spiced, this is the classic Indian chai with Mission warmth. Infused with ginger, pepper, cinnamon and cardamom, it's perfect hot or iced.

INGREDIENTS

For the prep
1 l oat or full-fat cow's milk
15 g black tea
40 g fresh sliced ginger
2 g crushed black pepper
1 g crushed cardamom
1 cinnamon stick (crushed)
50 g sugar

Garnish
1 star anise
sprinkle of cinnamon powder

METHOD

Add all the ingredients to a pan. Heat gently for 15 minutes. Bring to a boil and reduce the heat. Let simmer for another 15 minutes.

Strain before serving.

To serve hot
Pour straight into a teacup, garnish and enjoy.

To serve iced
Let it cool in the fridge, then pour over two large ice cubes.

Summer tip: Make chai ice cubes so you don't water down your drink. Just pour cooled chai into an ice tray, freeze, and use when serving iced.

Flavour profile	serves	Glass
sweet/creamy	6	tall glass

मानगो लस्सी

MANGO LASSI

The original smoothie. Creamy yoghurt blended with ripe mango, full-fat milk, sugar, and a touch of green cardamom. A classic cooler – and the perfect pairing with a spicy meal. It's an easy recipe to switch out ingredients like yoghurt and milk for a plant-based alternative.

INGREDIENTS

For the prep
500 ml full-fat yoghurt
340 ml mango purée (from 3 sweet, peeled mangoes)
300 ml full-fat milk
50 g sugar
1 g green cardamom powder

Garnish
lime wheel
sugar-coated fennel seeds

METHOD

Stir all drink ingredients together until smooth and well combined. Serve chilled in a tall glass.
Garnish and enjoy.

Winter tip: No fresh mango? Use frozen mango or swap in another ripe fruit like banana, peach or pineapple.
Add a shot of your favourite spirit for a drunken version.

Flavour profile	*serves*	Glass
tangy/refreshing	*1*	long drink

इमली सोडा
IMLI SODA

Our favourite cocktail turned into a fizzy, tangy and sweet tamarind soda – a refreshing twist on Indian-style cola.

INGREDIENTS

For the prep
lime
chilli salt (see below)
5 cl tamarind syrup (see below)
ice cubes
15 cl soda water

Garnish
fresh lime twist

METHOD

Rim the glass with lime and chilli salt.

Pour the tamarind syrup into the glass. Fill the glass with ice cubes and top it with the soda water. Stir well.

Garnish and serve.

TAMARIND SYRUP

Combine 300 ml water, 200 g sugar, and 100 g seedless tamarind in a pan.

Bring to a boil and simmer for 10 minutes.

Strain, cool and store in the fridge.

CHILLI SALT

Mix ¾ part coarse salt with ¼ part chili flakes.

Use to rim glasses for spicy cocktails or sprinkle over fruit for a little extra heat.

FIREWATER
BUY
MISSION RUM
HERE
FOR GIFTING
OR DRINKING
Pineapple
·HOUSE BLEND·

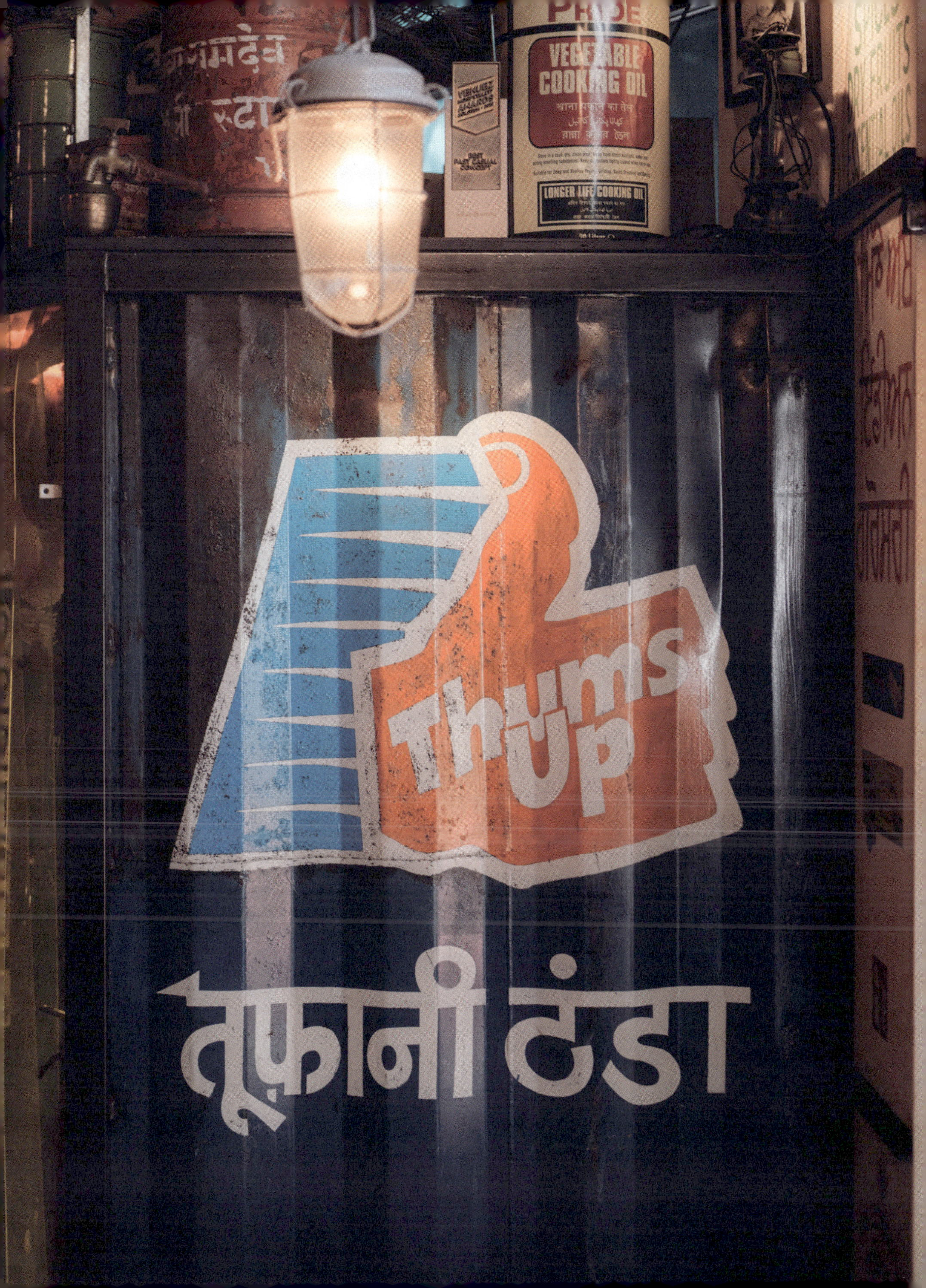

VEGETABLE
COOKING OIL
LONGER LIFE COOKING OIL
Thums Up
तूफ़ानी ठंडा

OUR SPOTS

Restaurants

1. MISSION MASALA ANTWERP
Where it all began. Indian soul food, street vibes, full heart.

2. BOMBAY BBQ BRUSSELS (Flagey)
Our flagship. Smoke, spice, fire, and the Gault&Millau "H!P of the Year" winner.

3. MISSION MASALA GHENT
Round two. Big flavours, bold energy, always packed.

4. KARMA KITCHEN BRUSSELS (Sainte Catherine)
In the heart of the city, our ode to southern coastal travels.

5. CURRY CLUB WOLF FOOD MARKET ANTWERP & BRUSSELS
Foodtruck style menus served from a fixed kiosk in a bustling foodcourt.

Take out and delivery

Our invitation to share the joy, colour and rhythm of street food and the way we mix flavours.

6. CURRY CLUB ANTWERP & BRUSSELS
Born out of necessity, designed for delivery.

1

2

3

5

4

6

Tag us at @missionmasala_bombaybbq
Share your creations with #EatIndiaBook
See you online, or better yet, at the table.

And don't forget
↓ the playlist ↓

THANK YOU FOR EATING WITH US.

धन्यवाद

This book is more than a collection of recipes. It's an invitation to share the joy, colour and rhythm of street food and the way we mix flavours.

It's about everyone who's joined us, whether at our tables, from our food trucks or out of a takeaway box on the sofa.

What started as a side hustle on four wheels and two stubborn hearts has grown into something bigger than we ever imagined: a family, a movement, and a community we're endlessly grateful for.

To our teams, past and present, and to everyone who helped us turn an out-of-control hobby into this, thank you. We couldn't have done it without you.

And if you've cooked from these pages, you're part of the story. Even if you've just read them like a midnight menu, that counts too!

We hope these recipes bring flavour, joy and just enough mess into your kitchen, because that's where everything good begins.

With love,

Pavan, Tim & the Mission Family

www.lannoo.com
Register on our web site and we will regularly send you a newsletter with information about new books and interesting, exclusive offers.

Text: Pavan Bajwa
Photography: Studio Legein, (except p. 4, 194, 195, 201 – Eat Dust, p. 197 – Gilles Draps)
Design: Olivier Smets

If you have observations or questions, please contact our editorial office: redactielifestyle@lannoo.com

D/2025/45/598 – NUR 440, 442
ISBN 9789059960657

Special thanks to:

Our hardcore HQ team Guido, Emma, Lotte, Bent & Roel

Our creative master mind Olivier Smets

Our head chefs Dafna & Raja

OG Chef Toon De Bock

Curry mafia & spice royalty: Papa Micki (Nana ji) & Mama Mo (Nani ji)

The support foundation: Dadi Ma Simonne & Babba Ji Noël

Saskia @ The Wicked PR

Eat Dust & G.O.D for the drip

Perfect painters Hans a.k.a. Señor Color & François Tusseki

Camera Kings Bas Van Hoof, Nicolas @ Studio Legein & Gilles Draps

Construction & Decoration Valentijn Hutte, William De Wandeler & Pavel Van Oost

All our friends that supported & helped us all the way!

Every single team member a.k.a. The United Colors Of Mission Masala

Our every day sunshine Uma Kaur!

Our Suppliers & Partners in Food:

Femke & Kobe + team @ Kolonel Coffee

Peter & Maggi @ Socal Taco's

John @ OldBoy

Mathieu @ Swet

Lynn & David from Camino

Leaders Club

Michele @ Pukkelpop

Denis @ Horeca Totaal

The team @ Geyskens

Global Choice Foods

Liesbeth, Geert & Sander @ Zilverberg Food

Lester @ World's End Rum

Dok Brewing Company

Katleen @ Atelier 147

Maarten & Seba @ Semtech

Rudy @ De Prol Consulting

Cédric @ Fernand Obb

David @ De Zuivelarij

The team @ Uber Eats

Michiel & Sebastiaan @ Wolf Food Market

André & Roelien @ Hop Producties

Roeland Fort Wines

AAPI

HorecaFocus

Growzer

Joris @ Neonart

Biopack

Jean Sur Mer (RIP)

Delidis

Odas

Jobkitchen

Jurgen @ P&V

Studio Calypso & Peace Of Cake Agency

Dennis @ Master Chef Belgium

Chloe @ Brussels Kitchen

WEIGHTS FOR DRY INGREDIENTS

20g	¾ oz
25g	1 oz
40g	1½oz
50g	2oz
60g	2½oz
75g	3oz
100g	3½oz
125g	4oz
150g	5oz
175g	6oz
200g	7oz
225g	8oz
250g	9oz
300g	11oz
350g	12oz
400g	14oz
450g	1lb
500g	1lb 2oz
550g	1¼lb
600g	1lb 5oz
650g	1lb 7oz
700g	1lb 9oz
750g	1lb 11oz
800g	1¾lb
900g	2lb
1kg	2¼lb

LIQUID MEASURES

METRIC	IMPERIAL	US
25ml	1fl oz	
50ml	2fl oz	¼ cup
75ml	3fl oz	
100ml	3½fl oz	
120ml	4fl oz	½ cup
150ml	5fl oz	
175ml	6fl oz	¾ cup
200ml	7fl oz	
250ml	8fl oz	1 cup
300ml	10fl oz/½ pint	1¼ cups
400ml	14fl oz	
450ml	15fl oz	2 cups/1 pint
600ml	1 pint	2½ cups
750ml	1¼ pints	
900ml	1½ pints	
1 litre	1¾ pints	1 quart

OVEN TEMPERATURES

°C	°F
110	225
120	250
140	275
150	300
160	325
180	350
190	375
200	400
220	425
230	450
240	475

MISSION MASALA
मिशन मसाला
EAT INDIA

आ रहा है

LIP KUMAR
INI KAUSHAL
IN

सुजितकुमार
हेलेन
जीवन

Desi

ईस्टमनकलर

भोजपुरी में

संगीत

आनंद बक्षी

के. एच. काप

रत्ना फिल्मस कार्पोरेशन